Physical Education for Young Children

Movement ABCs for the Little Ones

Rae Pica

Human Kinetics

Library of Congress Cataloging-in-Publication Data

Pica, Rae, 1953-
   Physical education for young children : movement ABCs for the little ones / Rae Pica.
     p. cm.
   Includes bibliographical references and index.
   ISBN-13: 978-0-7360-7149-9 (soft cover)
   ISBN-10: 0-7360-7149-0 (soft cover)
   1. Physical education for children. 2. Movement education. I. Title.
   GV443.P485 2008
   372.86--dc22
                                    2008024605
   ISBN-10: 0-7360-7149-0
   ISBN-13: 978-0-7360-7149-9

Copyright © 2008 by Rae Pica

The Web addresses cited in this text were current as of May 2008, unless otherwise noted.

Acquisitions Editor: Scott Wikgren; **Developmental Editor:** Ray Vallese; **Assistant Editor:** Derek Campbell; **Copyeditor:** Annette Pierce; **Proofreader:** Coree Clark; **Indexer:** Sharon Duffy; **Permission Manager:** Carly Breeding; **Graphic Designer:** Nancy Rasmus; **Graphic Artist:** Denise Lowry; **Cover Designer:** Keith Blomberg; **Photographer (cover):** Keith Blomberg; **Photographer (interior):** Neil Bernstein, unless otherwise noted; photos on pages 1, 3, 8, 11, 31, 43, 63, 77, and 89 © Human Kinetics; photo on page 71 © Art Explosion; photo on page 131 is courtesy of Rae Pica; **Photo Asset Manager:** Laura Fitch; **Visual Production Assistant:** Joyce Brumfield; **Photo Office Assistant:** Jason Allen; **Art Manager:** Kelly Hendren; **Associate Art Manager:** Alan L. Wilborn; **Illustrator:** Keri Evans; **Printer:** Total Printing Systems

Printed in the United States of America   10 9 8 7 6 5 4 3 2

The paper in this book is certified under a sustainable forestry program.

Human Kinetics
Website: www.HumanKinetics.com

United States: Human Kinetics, P.O. Box 5076, Champaign, IL 61825-5076
800-747-4457
e-mail: humank@hkusa.com

Canada: Human Kinetics, 475 Devonshire Road Unit 100, Windsor, ON N8Y 2L5
800-465-7301 (in Canada only)
e-mail: info@hkcanada.com

Europe: Human Kinetics, 107 Bradford Road, Stanningley, Leeds LS28 6AT, United Kingdom
+44 (0) 113 255 5665
e-mail: hk@hkeurope.com

Australia: Human Kinetics, 57A Price Avenue, Lower Mitcham, South Australia 5062
08 8372 0999
e-mail: info@hkaustralia.com

New Zealand: Human Kinetics, P.O. Box 80, Torrens Park, South Australia 5062
0800 222 062
e-mail: info@hknewzealand.com

E4233

This book is dedicated to the memory of Lucille Page West,
whose adult dance class changed the direction of my life and work,
and to Rainer Martens, founder and president of Human Kinetics,
whose decision to publish me 20 years ago
brought my life's work full circle.

Contents

Preface

The question I'm most often asked by elementary school physical education teachers, in one form or another, is "What am I supposed to do with the little ones?" Despite all the training they've had, many PE teachers are stumped when it comes to the developmental needs and abilities of young children. And it makes perfect sense. The majority of college preparation programs don't address the issue of early childhood physical education, in part, I suspect, because public kindergarten and especially preschool have not been part of school systems for very long, meaning PE for preschoolers and kindergartners is a more recent development. Also, I imagine the university curriculum designers believe that methods courses for *elementary* physical education sufficiently tackle the topic of what to do with the little ones.

The problem, however—as those of you suddenly faced with the reality of preschool and kindergarten classes have discovered—is that the "little ones" are a whole different animal from what you've been taught to expect of elementary school students. Moreover, because children up to the age of eight are, developmentally speaking, more like their younger counterparts than like upper elementary children, much of what you learned in elementary methods classes doesn't necessarily apply even to the first- through third-graders.

As evidence of the confusion surrounding the content of physical education for early elementary grades, a middle school PE teacher recently attended one of my workshops with the intention of learning what it is students should be able to do by the time they enter his gym. He was concerned, he said, because they didn't seem to be able to *do* much of anything—and he knew that shouldn't be the case!

What *should* students ages four to eight be expected to do physically? What should their physical education program look like?

You'll find the answers to those questions in *Physical Education for Young Children: Movement ABCs for the Little Ones*. But I can give you the short answer to the latter question here: The focus of early childhood and early elementary PE programs should be on the fundamentals. It seems simple enough. But maybe that's the problem, because when I explain this to PE teachers, even those who are already focusing on the fundamentals worry that it just isn't enough.

Most PE professionals, after all, enter the field because physical activity is something they're good at. Having excelled in sports, dance, or gymnastics, they want their students to become similarly skilled. They want physical activity to play as large a role in the children's lives as it has in theirs. With that in mind, it's hard to imagine that emphasizing such things as body and spatial awareness or basic locomotor and nonlocomotor skills will achieve the desired goal.

If you've had these same concerns, it might be helpful to ponder the questions I've posed to parents eager to enroll their little ones in adult-style sports:

- Would you expect a child to do calculus problems once she was able to count to 10?
- Would you hand a child a geometry text once he began to recognize shapes?
- Do you imagine a child could read *War and Peace* simply because she's mastered her ABCs?
- Would you send a child to high school before he'd attended elementary and middle schools?

Obviously, the answer to all of these questions is "Of course not!" Parents recognize the preposterousness of these expectations. Unfortunately, they tend not to realize that the same considerations apply to their children's physical development. Too many parents don't think twice about enrolling their young children in gymnastics, karate, dance classes, and organized sports before their kids have mastered basics such as body-part identification, walking with correct posture, and bouncing and catching a ball. How is that significantly different, for example, from expecting a child who has barely learned to speak to clearly recite the Declaration of Independence—for an audience, no less?

Along those same lines, as a PE professional, it's important to realize that because a little one can walk, it doesn't necessarily mean she's ready to successfully—or fearlessly—walk a balance beam. Because a preschooler is flexible enough to get his big toe to his chin, it doesn't mean he's ready for tumbling stunts. Even if a five-year-old can run circles around you, it doesn't mean she's prepared to simultaneously run and dribble a ball in a game of soccer. And how much sense does it make to ask an eight-year-old to pitch when he's still demonstrating an immature throwing form?

Simply put, children still in the early childhood stage—defined by the National Association for the Education of Young Children (NAEYC) as birth to age eight—are not yet developmentally ready to participate in organized sports, traditional gymnastics or dance, or even overly structured games—the staples of a typical physical education program and probably the primary content of your college courses.

ABCs of Movement

Movements—from the simple to the complex—are like building blocks. We must lay the foundation before we can construct the ground floor. We have to complete the ground floor before we can erect the rest of the building. Similarly, a logical progression of movement skills is essential if children are to achieve optimal physical and motor development. If they skip the prerequisites, they may never progress successfully from one level of skill development to the next.

What are the prerequisites? I call them the ABCs of movement: body-part identification, basic motor skills (nonlocomotor, locomotor, and manipulative), and awareness of the elements of movement (space, shape, time, force, flow, and rhythm). Just as you wouldn't expect children to begin reading without the ability to identify the letters of the alphabet, you shouldn't expect children to take part in highly structured or challenging physical activities without first experiencing success with the ABCs of movement.

In other words, put fundamentals first. Children should walk before they run. They should bend and stretch before they twist and dodge. They should throw for distance before throwing for accuracy. Static movement such as balancing on tiptoes or hitting a ball off a tee should precede dynamic movements such as walking a balance beam or hitting a pitched ball. And children should definitely succeed at single actions such as bouncing a ball before attempting combinations of them such as simultaneously running and bouncing a ball. Children who first master the fundamentals are far more likely to feel confident about their movement abilities and therefore continue moving throughout their lives.

In this book, I begin with a look at what you can expect—or *not* expect—developmentally from young children. Chapter 1 covers the highlights of physical, social-emotional, and cognitive development as they pertain to the teaching of physical education. Chapter 2 then helps you understand how to use what you know about young children to create and maintain a positive atmosphere in the gym. Prekindergarten to third-grade students simply can't be expected to file in, take their places, and wait quietly; nor can they be expected to participate in a manner similar to older students. Chapter 2 can help you to adjust your expectations accordingly and to teach young students in ways that ensure success.

The next three chapters are dedicated to the ABCs of movement. Chapter 3 explores the elements of movement—sometimes referred to as movement concepts—with which young children should become familiar and comfortable. Chapter 4 looks at the progression involved in the acquisition of motor skills, followed by a description of locomotor and nonlocomotor movements and the ways in which the movement elements can be used to help children acquire and refine these skills. Then, because promoting lifelong fitness should be the goal of every PE program, chapter 5 covers the ABCs as part of a developmentally appropriate fitness plan for the little ones. It's my intention to show that teaching the fundamentals and promoting fitness don't have to be mutually exclusive endeavors.

The manipulative skills, which have traditionally received the greatest amount of attention in PE programs, are addressed in chapter 6. I have purposely addressed these skills later in the book because, developmentally speaking, young children should first master basic locomotor and nonlocomotor skills before focusing on the manipulation of objects.

In chapter 7, because the three developmental domains (physical, social-emotional, and cognitive) are especially interrelated in early childhood and because young children cannot learn something in one domain without it affecting the others, I've offered information on using movement across the curriculum. Linking the gym with the classroom makes the activities you ask the children to do more relevant to their lives and generates greater enthusiasm among your students. It has the added benefit of helping PE professionals—many of whom are increasingly in the position of having to do so—to serve as advocates for their field.

Finally, appendix A provides you with sample lesson plans and appendix B with resources for children's music, equipment and props, professional organizations, and Web sites.

Fun and Success

Chances are, you don't recall your earliest movement experiences, and it's unlikely they took place within the context of a physical education class. Rather, they probably occurred as part of your daily play, much of which took place outdoors. As you know, outdoor, gross motor play is a dying art among today's young children, who spend much of their time in sedentary indoor activities. That means that many of their early movement experiences will take place in your gym. It's critical, therefore, that the children experience both fun and success in the gym if you want physical activity to continue to be part of their lives. Because although most children begin life with a love of movement, if their early physical experiences involve more frustration and failure than fun and success, love of movement can rapidly disappear.

Remember: Not every child who enters your gym will be as physically skilled or as enamored of physical activity as you probably were when you were his or her age. It's difficult to imagine, I know, but it's true—especially in today's society, where so many electronic options compete for the child's time and attention. With that in mind, you need to offer these young students *challenges that are equal to the skills they possess.* Otherwise, anxiety and learned helplessness (the expectation, based on past experience, that one's every effort will lead to failure) are the likely results. And if that happens, you may end up creating more lifelong couch potatoes than physically active people.

A PE professor recently told me that her students frequently declare that they hate it when the kindergartners come in to the gym. I wasn't surprised to hear it. After all, when you signed on to be a physical education professional it's likely you had visions of helping children become both fit and athletically inclined. You wanted to teach them to do all the things at which you're so skilled. Teaching them to understand their own personal space, to be unafraid to catch a ball, or to walk with correct posture probably never crossed your mind!

But if you can look at it in a different way, if you can understand that you're providing the most important physical education of all—the *foundation* for a lifetime of physical activity and fitness—you'll be thrilled to see those little ones coming. Think *fun* and *success* with your littlest students, and you'll give them the best possible start toward a lifelong love of movement. And in the process, you'll experience fun and success as well.

Acknowledgments

I want to offer my sincere thanks to the Human Kinetics family, especially acquisitions editor Scott Wikgren, for his support and for being such a great guy; my developmental editor, Ray Vallese, for his attention to detail and his enthusiasm for the project; and assistant editor Derek Campbell, also for his attention to detail and for being so easy to work with. I'm grateful to all the teachers and children with whom I've worked over the past 28 years and who have taught me so much. Last, but certainly not least, I offer my gratitude and love to the special people who offer me "life support," among them my husband, Richard Gardzina, my business partner and kindred spirit, Errol Smith, and longtime friends Sheila Chapman and Patti Page.

What Your
College Courses
Didn't Tell You

As mentioned in the preface, children in the early childhood period are quite unlike older children. They think differently, they act differently, and their feelings are right on the surface and not yet under control. And not to be ignored, their physical development is still in the beginning stages.

Although this book isn't the place for a complete overview of early childhood development, this chapter touches on the salient points of the physical, social-emotional, and cognitive development of young children—the points most applicable to teaching physical education.

Physical Domain

Children *look* like small adults, so it is perhaps in the **physical domain** that we're most likely to err, expecting more from those little people than they're capable of doing. Yes, they have the same body parts and the same number of them that their older counterparts have, so it's easy to assume that with a little practice they'll be able to perform the same skills executed by older children. But should we ask them to do so? This is when reality hits: The little ones *can't* perform the same skills. And it's not just a matter of practice; rather, there's a whole lot happening on the inside developmentally that precludes young children from performing as we may expect them to.

- Eye–hand coordination
- Eye–foot coordination
- Figure–ground perception
- Depth perception
- Peripheral vision
- Visual–motor coordination

Figure 1.1 Visual skills are not fully developed in early childhood.

To begin, several factors relative to vision affect the children's performance in the gym (see figure 1.1). They include the following:

• Eye–hand and eye–foot coordination usually aren't fully developed until the age of 9 or 10. How, then, is a child of four or five to successfully connect bat to ball, stick to puck, or foot to moving soccer ball?

• **Figure–ground perception**—the ability to separate or distinguish an object from its surroundings—reaches maturity from ages of 8 to 12. This means, for example, that a young child trying to throw a ball or beanbag through an upright hoop will have trouble differentiating the hoop from its background.

• **Depth perception**—the ability to judge distance in relation to oneself—is generally not mature until age 12. A child with immature depth perception will be unable to accurately judge the distance of an oncoming object, like a thrown or batted ball, which is why so many young children are afraid of them (see figure 1.2). Preschoolers also run into objects and each other because of immature depth perception. This means that, whenever possible, their paths must be kept clear, and they must be allowed enough time to change directions. By age seven, children should be able to travel freely throughout a room without collisions.

- **Peripheral vision,** which refers to the ability to see things to the side while the eyes are focused on a central point, doesn't mature until the teenage years. Consider the need to be aware of other players in games or team sports or to avoid surrounding objects like trees or bleachers, and you'll understand the importance of peripheral vision.

- **Visual–motor coordination**—the ability to integrate the use of the eyes and hands in terms of object tracking—matures from ages 10 to 12. Although infants are able to visually track slowly moving objects, it isn't until about age 12 that children can make fast and accurate judgments about quickly moving objects. Consider the visual tracking required when an eight-year-old soccer goalie tries to intercept an approaching ball. First she has to locate the ball, which may require her to reposition her body. She must also quickly determine the ball's distance, speed, and angle of approach and predict where it will arrive and how long it will take to get there. Almost simultaneously, "she must plan and then implement a movement response so that she gets to the intercept point on time and is positioned so that she can catch, kick, or deflect the ball to prevent it from

Figure 1.2 Young children are often afraid of a thrown ball because their depth perception is not yet fully developed.

crossing the goal line" (Haubenstricker and Seefeldt, 2002, pp. 67-68). If that seems ambitious for an eight-year-old, consider the possibilities for success when a preschooler tries to defend the net!

Beyond the visual realities is the fact that a young child is still growing. The typical child grows three inches and gains 10 pounds from the ages of five to seven, but that's just what we can see on the outside. This growth process includes muscles, joints, bones, and organs, all of which can be negatively affected by impact sports. Body *scale* also plays a major role. Changes in the size of body parts in relation to one another can have a tremendous impact on strength, coordination, and balance. The size of a preschooler's head, for instance, is reason enough for concern. It's the largest part of his body and, proportionally, has been likened to an adult having a head the size of a beach ball. It's a funny image but probably not all that humorous to the frustrated five-year-old trying to keep his balance and coordinate his movements as he tries to wield a bat, turn the corner at first base, or kick a fast-moving ball.

Despite the size of the head, balance shows tremendous improvement during the preschool years. Three-year-olds can balance only briefly on the preferred foot and walk a low balance beam with adult assistance. By the time they're four, most preschoolers hop successfully on the dominant foot and on the nondominant foot by about four-and-a-half. At age five, children usually can manage the balance beam by themselves and stand on one foot with hands on hips for 10 seconds or longer (Skinner, 1979).

If you work with six-year-olds, you know they're generally able to run, jump, and bounce and catch a ball, all of which can be considered sport skills. Still, these children haven't yet had the instruction, practice, and experience required to perform these skills at a *mature* level, which means they aren't likely to perform them well enough to be successful in sports or highly structured games. In fact, according to a study conducted at Northern Kentucky University, 49 percent of the 1,100 five- to eight-year-olds surveyed were found to lack the ability to perform even the most fundamental skills required in their sports (Bach, 1997).

Motor development is not age dependent; rather, it is merely age related. Figure 1.3 highlights some of the milestones in gross motor development, but they are general guidelines only.

❓ CONSIDER THIS

A child's control over his or her body develops from the top to the bottom. The ability to move the head comes most easily then progresses down to the toes. It develops from the inside to the outside—from the trunk to extremities—and from gross motor movement of the trunk, neck, arms, and legs to fine motor movement of the hands, fingers, wrists, toes, and eyes.

Three to Four Years
- Changes speed, direction, or style of movement at signal
- Walks a straight line and low balance beam
- Runs on tiptoes
- Throws objects without losing balance, can throw underarm
- Gallops
- Hops briefly
- Uses alternating feet to ascend stairs
- Catches a large or bounced ball with both arms extended
- Jumps to the floor from approximately 12 inches (30 centimeters)
- Performs a forward roll

Four to Five Years
- Better able to start, stop, turn, and move around obstacles and other people
- Hops on nondominant foot
- Crosses feet over midline of body
- Descends stairs with alternating feet
- Jumps over objects five to six inches (13 to 15 centimeters) high
- Leaps over objects 10 inches (25 centimeters) high
- Bounces and catches a ball
- Sometimes skips on one side only
- Performs a backward roll
- Throws with basic overarm pattern
- Catches by trapping ball to chest

Five to Six Years
- Slides
- Skips using alternating feet
- Catches a thrown ball with hands, although not always successfully
- Balances on either foot
- Shifts weight to throw (steps out with foot opposite the throwing hand)
- Kicks a rolling ball
- Bounces a ball with one hand

Six to Eight Years
- Performs most gross motor skills
- Executes two skills concurrently (for example, walking and bouncing)
- Learns simple folk and partner dances

Figure 1.3 Motor milestones.

A child takes significant steps from the time she's an infant until she's a preschooler—literally—moving from a prone position to being upright and soon after being able to run and jump. But it's a mistake to imagine that the child can do any of these things *well*. Preschoolers are just learning to identify what and where their body parts are and haven't really begun learning how to use them. Using them in a coordinated fashion is simply asking too much.

Social-Emotional Domain

Each year of physical growth during the preschool stage shows a corresponding growth in self-awareness, self-confidence, and self-control, all areas related to the **social-emotional domain,** also known as affective development. At the same time, preschoolers show increasing interest and concern for one another, learning to take turns (on a limited basis and only if they don't have to wait very long), share, and collaborate.

Although research has shown that preschool children prefer cooperative activities to competitive ones, one study indicates that in the United States, gender identity, which is typically established by the age of three, plays a role in whether children are naturally cooperative or competitive (Garcia, 1994). Preschool girls, according to the study, are cooperative, caring, and supportive of one another when learning new movement skills. They're not interested in competing or succeeding at someone else's expense and actually seem to learn less efficiently when competition is introduced.

Preschool boys, on the other hand, are interested in how well they perform and in how their abilities compare with those of their classmates. However, the study further indicates that the differences in the boys' and girls' behavior may actually be dictated by society and culture: Asian preschoolers of both genders tended to be cooperative and supportive. This is substantiated by an essay in the *New York Times*, in which Nicholas Kristof

? CONSIDER THIS

Putting preschoolers in game situations that oblige them to interact in ways they don't understand won't teach them cooperative skills. Because they're still in the egocentric stage, they will be confused by the request to pass the soccer ball to a teammate, throw the baseball to the first baseman, or to hand off the football to the running back. These items are *their* precious possessions, and they don't want to relinquish them.

(1998) told the story of trying to teach the game of musical chairs to a group of five-year-old Japanese children, who politely stepped out of the way so their peers could have their seats.

Developmentally speaking, learning to cooperate must precede learning to compete, because young children aren't ready for the concepts involved in organized play and teamwork. But because egocentrism (being centered on self) doesn't begin to decline until age seven or eight, you should wait until your students are about five before introducing simple cooperative partner and group activities.

If you've worked with preschoolers, you have noticed that they show an eagerness to please you, and all adults, in fact, and are particularly susceptible to praise. Four-year-olds, specifically, often seek adult approval, and five-year-olds show a special fondness for their teachers. During the early elementary years, children demonstrate a growing interest in peers. Although they still respond to adult approval, in the primary grades peer acceptance becomes a stronger force than adult acceptance. From the ages of six to eight, children begin to compare themselves with others.

During this period gender awareness also begins to play a role. Children from six to eight generally will play with others of the same sex, particularly in small groups. They may not choose partners of the opposite sex, but if assigned to each other for an activity, they still seem to enjoy it. Boys tend to be more concerned with sex-role stereotypes than girls are.

Of special significance is the fact that, for young children, *process* matters far more than *product*. In physical activity, the process is in the playing. Young children don't care about winning, which is an adult concept, nor about how well they're playing unless the important adults in their lives make it clear that they care about those things.

Although the emphasis should remain on process through the primary grades, early elementary students will become increasingly interested in the final product. Task completion and success contribute to their feelings of self-esteem, with fears associated with achievement, or lack thereof, common between the ages of 6 and 11 (Charlesworth, 2008). A desire to excel typically begins in the second and third grades. Students in these grades like to be admired for doing things well.

 CONSIDER THIS

PE and motor development experts contend that children should experience an 80 percent success rate during physical activities. If they don't, scale back the challenges.

Cognitive Domain

We can't see all that's occurring physically, and we *really* can't know everything going on inside the heads of young children (the **cognitive domain**). From the ages of about two to seven years old, children function at what noted child development expert Jean Piaget called the *preoperational stage of thinking.* This means that, unlike adults and older children, they're not yet able to think logically or abstractly and are able to handle only one aspect of a problem at a time.

In terms of physical education, that means children up to the age of seven are unable to decipher complicated coaching instructions, rules, or strategies or to contemplate doing two things at once. For example, during a game of soccer, a preschooler will become so focused on dribbling (or trying to) that he'll be unable to even consider the possibility of passing the ball to a teammate. "One thought at a time" might well be the young child's credo, as is obvious to anyone who's ever witnessed what's been called "beehive" or "big-clump" soccer in which the children swarm or move together in one big group because they're exclusively concentrated on following the ball (see figure 1.4). This all-too-common occurrence is also a prime example of the young child's inability to comprehend instructions and strategies. They don't possess the ability to understand until around age 10.

Figure 1.4   "Big-clump" or "beehive" soccer is an example of the young child's ability to focus on only one idea at a time.

Add to this the "space cadet" syndrome, i.e., the distractibility, exhibited by the typical preschooler, and you have a child who is easily sidetracked and periodically loses interest in what's going on around her. A few children of this age may be reasonably focused, but they're the exception rather than the rule. The rule is that most children under the age of eight have an attention span that can be measured in moments, and the adult who understands that this is a developmental stage will be far less frustrated than the adult who expects children to be as focused as he or she may be.

Children under the age of eight also require time to consider the movements they want to make. That's because their decision-making abilities are noticeably slower than those of older children and adults. This means they're not only performing movements more slowly than those who have had years of practice, but also they're taking more time to think about the movements. Another relevant point is that the younger the preschoolers, the more time they'll need to organize themselves as a group. This is especially important to remember if you're planning activities that arrange the children in circles, lines, or other formations.

You should also be aware that young children can hold only two or three items at a time in their working memory, as compared with the adolescent or adult, who can retain five to nine items. So if you rattle off a list of instructions, there's little chance the children will even be listening by the time you're finished. Chances are also good that they won't understand all the words you rattled off anyway because their language capacity is still limited.

Not only do they know the meaning of fewer words, but young children also are quite literal in their interpretations. Darrell Burnett, in *It's Just a Game!* (2001), describes two examples of this: the child whose coach told him to "cover second base" and therefore threw his body over the bag, and the seven-year-old whose father told him to "mark his man" during the soccer game and therefore picked up some dirt and rubbed it on an opponent's shoulder! These incidents aren't rare exceptions, and they're certainly not intended to aggravate you. Rather, they're examples of children acting like children and why it's so important to understand them.

When children reach the early elementary grades, their increased levels of problem-solving and communication skills open up new possibilities for your PE program. First, you can present a wider range of divergent and convergent problem-solving challenges to early elementary children (see chapter 2). And, by doing so, you'll promote critical-thinking skills and help children learn how to learn. You can test and stretch children's verbal skills by soliciting their ideas and feedback. Also, by presenting children with challenges that require interaction between partners or among group members, you can promote both problem solving *and* communication skills.

➡ REMEMBER THIS

Knowing what you can and cannot expect from children ages four to eight can make all the difference in how much they learn from you during these early years. And because these are formative years, the experiences you choose to offer can make the difference in whether or not your young students later become couch potatoes or active for life.

- Many visual abilities that are significant to sports do not mature until late childhood or adolescence.
- The muscles, joints, bones, and organs of a young child are still growing and forming, and body scale is still disproportional.
- By the time children are six, they're generally able to perform several of the skills involved in sports and formal games, but they haven't had enough instruction, practice, and experience to perform them well.
- Children aren't typically ready to understand the perspective of another person until age seven or eight.
- Process is far more important than product in a young child's life. Winning is a product and an adult concept.
- Children from the ages of two to seven aren't able to think logically or abstractly, which means they can't decipher involved instructions, rules, or strategies.
- The decision-making abilities of young children are noticeably slower than those of older children and adults.

2

Maintaining a Successful Learning Environment

If you dread seeing the little ones come into the gym, it's likely due to unrealistic expectations of their physical abilities *and* their behavior. For example, you probably want them to listen, to take direction, and to be reasonably quiet and well managed. You certainly don't expect them to be bouncing off the walls.

Well, chances are that of all the characteristics cited in the previous paragraph, bouncing off the walls is the one at which they're best. But that doesn't mean you have to end each class tearing out your hair and wishing you'd chosen a different profession. If you understand how the little ones operate—and how they don't—and you start from where the children are, rather than from where you'd like them to be, you'll experience more satisfaction than frustration.

In this chapter we look at the children's physical starting point: body-part identification. We then review how their cognitive traits relate to the teaching methods you choose. Finally, we address the social-emotional issue of class management—how to keep them from bouncing off the walls (most of the time anyway).

Beginning With the Body

Body-part identification may seem too simplistic to be part of a physical education curriculum, but it's actually where physical, or movement, education begins for young children. Before children can learn how to use their body parts, especially in a coordinated fashion, they have to know what and where they are.

Preschoolers are just learning to identify what and where their body parts are. By age seven, the majority of children know their large and small parts. Still, many a student has arrived in the early elementary and even upper elementary grades not knowing, for example, his elbows from his shoulders. When such a child stands at home plate and is instructed to raise his elbows to improve his batting stance, he's likely to lift his shoulders toward his ears, which does nothing to help him hit the ball. If he's in a situation where he's expected to quickly respond to a teacher's or coach's instruction involving body parts, taking the time to think about what he's being asked to do could make the difference between success and failure in a game situation.

Reinforcing body-part identification, therefore, is a great starting point, which will result in immediate and future success for your students. Fortunately, there are numerous body-part activities and games you can conduct with preschool and early elementary kids. The following are just some of the possibilities.

Head, Belly, Toes

With the youngest students, the fewer body parts involved, the better the chance for success. Among the simplest of body-part identification activities are Head, Belly, Toes and Head, Shoulders, Knees, and Toes (the latter is more difficult because it involves more—and more challenging—body parts). With either of these activities, you call out the names of the body parts and the students touch the part you call out. Start slowly, saying the parts in the same order each time. Then, as the children gain experience, vary the tempo and the order. Once the children are ready for an additional challenge, begin calling out the body parts very slowly and gradually increase the pace. This also familiarizes them with the continuum from slow to fast, which is known in musical terms as *accelerando.*

Show Me

With preschoolers, you can play Show Me, in which you invite students to show you their various body parts, such as nose, toes, fingers, knees, ears, and legs. Body parts that may be more challenging for them to identify include shoulders, elbows, wrists, hips, shins, and ankles. As with Head, Belly, Toes, eventually increasing the tempo at which you call out body parts increases the challenge.

Simon Says

Simon Says, of course, is the perfect body-part identification game, once children are ready to grasp the concept and to listen carefully, and *if* it's played without the elimination process. The problem with playing it the traditional way is that the kids who most need to practice their body-part identification or listening skills or both are the first to be eliminated. Sitting against the wall and watching everybody else play does nothing to improve their skills.

The solution is a simple modification: Instead of playing the game with one large group, organize the children into two circles or lines. When a child moves without Simon's permission, she simply goes from one circle or line to the other, allowing for continual participation. To successfully play Simon Says with preschoolers and kindergartners, keep in mind that they're most likely to know the big body parts, like arms and legs. To increase the challenge for early elementary students, increase both the tempo at which you call out the commands and the complexity of the body parts. A forearm or a calf, for example, is more challenging than an arm or a leg. And a right or left forearm or calf is more challenging still, so this is best saved for your eight-year-olds.

Body Poem

Following is "The Body Poem." Start by reading it very slowly, with the children responding by pointing to, shaking, or wiggling the appropriate part or parts. The children can shrug on the last line of the third verse and move their hands the length of their bodies, from top to bottom and back again, on the next two lines. Repeat the poem several times, increasing the tempo with each repetition. Even if the children can't keep up with an exceptionally fast reading, they'll think it's hilarious and will look forward to performing the activity again and again. And because repetition is especially critical in early childhood, happy anticipation is a positive thing.

I have two feet

Two ears, two legs

Ten fingers and ten toes;

I have two knees,

Two lips, two hands,

And even two elbows;

I have two eyes

And four eyelids

So why, do you suppose,

With all these parts

On my body

I only have one nose?! (Pica, 2001)

Reprinted with permission from Gryphon House. Excerpted from "Wiggle, Giggle, & Shake," ISBN 978-0-87659-244-1. www.ghbooks.com. 800-638-0928.

Switcheroo

When the children are ready for the responsibility of cooperation, typically from five to seven years of age (although only you can judge their level of readiness), you can incorporate simple partner and group activities into the curriculum. A fun partner activity that reinforces body awareness is called Switcheroo. To play this game, the children stand back to back. When you call out the names of body parts, for example, "hands," the children turn to face each other, briefly touch those parts together, and then immediately return to their back-to-back positions. Continue by calling out a different set of body parts and occasionally, "switcheroo," which is the signal for children to switch partners.

The least challenging version of this game involves matching body parts (e.g., thumbs, knees, elbows, big toes, and wrists). Later, you can include nonmatching parts (e.g., a hand to a knee, a hand to a shoulder, a thumb to a big toe). Finally, once the children know their left from their right, generally by age eight, you can make the game the most challenging of all by calling out commands such as left hand to right knee, right thumb to right big toe, and so forth. Plan that this will take considerably more time; even adults are frequently stumped by these challenges.

 CONSIDER THIS

Before games in which children will have to change partners, designate the center of the room or gym as "lost and found." When children can't immediately find a new partner, they can go to this area to get one. This solves two problems: It alleviates the natural panic children feel at the idea of being left out, and it ensures you won't waste valuable class time while children search for partners.

Body-Part Boogie

With Body-Part Boogie, the children move when the music is playing and freeze when you pause it. The difference between this game and Statues (see page 39) is that you designate just one body part for them to move to the music, for example, an arm, a head, a foot, a leg, fingers. Of course, because young children find it difficult to isolate and use just one body part, you may at first find that *many* parts are moving as opposed to just the one you indicated. But that's okay, as long as they've included the part you indicated, you'll know they've correctly identified it.

Where Are My Body Parts?

One final activity—most appropriate for six- to eight-year-olds—involves working with a variety of body parts in relation to other body parts or to the floor. This requires that the children think a bit more about the sum of their parts and about the space they occupy (see figures 2.1 and 2.2).

Ask the children to sit, and then present challenges such as the following:

- Place a hand (or elbow) on the floor; move it as far from the floor as possible.
- Stretch a foot far away from you, and then bring it back to its original position.
- Put a shoulder (or the other shoulder or both shoulders) on the floor.

Figure 2.1 "Touch an elbow to a foot."

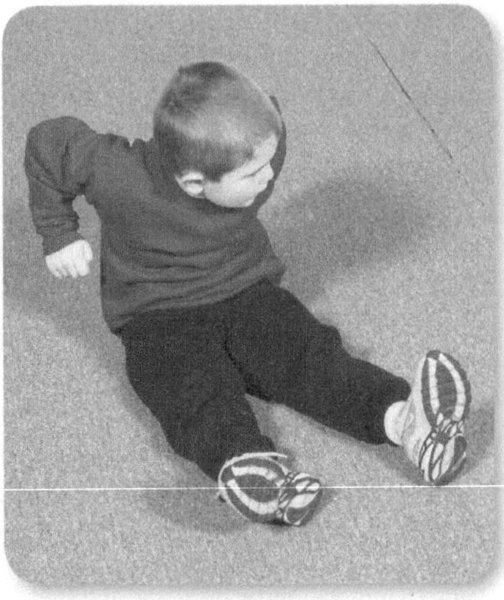

Figure 2.2 "Take your elbow as far away from your foot as possible."

- Touch an elbow to a knee; move it as far away from that knee as possible.
- Touch an elbow to a foot; move it as far away from that foot as possible.
- Rise up from the floor with your head leading and the rest of your body following.
- Return to the floor with an ear leading the way.
- Come back up with an elbow leading.

Summary of Activities

As you can see, most of these activities are stationary, which means they don't actively contribute to the development of gross motor skills or to cardiovascular fitness. They do, however, make wonderful warm-up or cool-down activities. Because many of them involve bending and stretching, or even twisting, they provide practice with these nonlocomotor skills and help develop flexibility, one of the health-related fitness factors. If performed while standing, they also can reinforce the concept of levels in space: low, middle, and high. In terms of making connections with the classroom curriculum, body-part identification falls under the content area of science, and cooperative activities contribute to social studies. The best part, however, is that young children enjoy these simple games, which means that the lessons learned as they play them will be meaningful and long lasting.

Teaching Methods

Traditionally, physical education has been taught using a command style of instruction. With this direct style, the teacher decides on the subject matter and how it's to be learned, and demonstration and imitation are the primary modes of instruction. Certainly this teaching style has its place and purpose and is addressed in the next section. But problem solving, both divergent and convergent, has much to offer young children in all three domains of development and should be a large part of your instructional approach. (Table 2.1 at the end of this section [page 23] cites some of the advantages and disadvantages of both the direct and indirect teaching styles.) We'll review the three teaching methods most appropriate for the little ones: the direct approach, movement exploration, and guided discovery.

Direct Approach

Some lessons and concepts simply lend themselves to the **direct approach** to teaching. In the human movement field, ballet is a prime example. This dance style consists of positions and steps that must be executed exactly, so expecting students to discover these positions and steps through exploration is a preposterous notion. Therefore, a command style that uses demonstration and imitation is the only teaching method that makes sense for ballet.

Although movements as codified as ballet steps are developmentally inappropriate for young children (with the exception of simple *pliés* and *relevés*), learning by imitation is sometimes appropriate and necessary. Modeling is often the best means of helping your youngest students and some children with special needs achieve success. Also, as children mature, they have to learn to follow directions and to physically imitate what their eyes see, for example, when they must write the letters of the alphabet they see in a book or on a chalkboard. These skills are "necessary ingredients of the early years" (Mosston and Ashworth, 1990, p. 45). Simon Says, Follow the Leader, mirroring, and songs accompanied by unison clapping or movement are examples of command-style activities that young children enjoy (see figure 2.3).

One advantage of this approach is that it produces immediate results. This, in turn, means you can instantly ascertain if a child is having difficulty following directions or executing the required response. For example, if the class is playing Simon Says and a child repeatedly touches the incorrect body part, you're alerted to a potential problem, possibly with hearing or processing information or simply with identifying body parts.

The efficient use of time is often seen as the most significant advantage of the direct approach. Naturally, it takes much less time to *show* the children how to perform movements than to let them discover how. And lack of

Figure 2.3   Playing a mirror game is a great way to familiarize students with the element of shape.

time is a common problem in physical education classes, which often last only 30 to 40 minutes.

Achieving conformity and uniformity are two of the behavior objectives—perpetuating traditional rituals is one of the subject-matter objectives—of the direct approach (Mosston and Ashworth, 1990). For example, if rituals like the Mexican Hat Dance and the Hokey Pokey are to be performed in a traditional manner—all the children doing the same thing at the same time—the only expedient way to teach these activities is with a direct approach, using demonstration and imitation. And because such activities are fun for young children and can produce a sense of belonging, they certainly should play a role in your program.

However, the early childhood years are commonly regarded as the best period for developing creativity. A major disadvantage of the direct approach is that it fails to allow for creativity and self-expression. Another disadvantage is that the direct approach doesn't allow for individual differences in development and ability among children. Finally, this style focuses on learning certain skills but not on the learning process itself (Gallahue, 1993). The direct approach, therefore, should play a lesser role in your program than do the indirect styles of movement exploration and guided discovery, which require students to solve problems.

Movement Exploration

Teaching methods that require students to solve problems are called indirect styles and are considered child centered, as opposed to teacher or task centered. **Movement exploration,** also known as **divergent problem solving,** is one such teaching style because each challenge can elicit a *variety* of correct responses. For example, a challenge to demonstrate crooked shapes can result in as many different crooked shapes as there are children responding (see figure 2.4). A challenge to balance on two body parts can result in one child balancing on the feet, another balancing on the knees, and still another, who may be enrolled in a gymnastics program, performing a handstand. Because this style helps promote critical- and creative-thinking skills and allows for individual differences among students, it is *the* most developmentally appropriate teaching method for the little ones.

Figure 2.4 "Show me a crooked shape."

Halsey and Porter wonderfully describe this instructional approach in their classic text, *Selected Readings in Movement Education* (1970, p. 76):

[Movement exploration] should follow such basic procedures as (1) setting the problem, (2) experimentation by the children, (3) observation and evaluation, (4) additional practice using points gained from evaluation. Answers to the problems, of course, are in movements rather than words. The movements will differ as individual children find the answer valid for each. The teacher does not demonstrate, encourage imitation, nor require any one best answer. Thus the children are not afraid to be different, and the teacher feels free to let them progress in their own way, each at his own rate. The result is a class atmosphere in which imagination has free play; invention becomes active and varied.

In other words, you'll present your students with a challenge (e.g., "Show me how tall you can be" or "Find two ways to move across the balance beam in a forward direction"), and the children will offer their responses in movement. You can issue additional challenges and vary the exploration by *extending* the activity (e.g., "Find another way" or "Show me you can also do it backward"). You also can issue follow-up questions and challenges intended to improve or correct what you've seen, known as *refining* responses. For example, if a child isn't getting on tiptoe when asked to reach as high as possible, ask "Can you use your feet to make yourself even taller?"

When extending activities, invite the students to continue finding new ideas until a pause occurs and the children appear momentarily stumped. Until then, even though students are producing divergent responses, they are mainly safe or common responses (Mosston and Ashworth, 1990). If you encourage the students to continue after the first pause, they'll have to find less common responses. If you persist in encouraging additional exploration beyond the second and third pauses, your students may often appear physically uncomfortable but eventually will cross the discovery or creativity threshold. New solutions evolve as divergent production continues. Of course, you'll have to design problems and suggest extensions that are developmentally appropriate and relevant to the subject matter and to the children's lives.

! TRY THIS

When expected to solve problems, children will first respond with the most obvious or common solution. As an example, when it gets down to a single chair while playing cooperative musical chairs, in which the children have been asked to share the remaining chairs, the most obvious solution is for one child to sit and the rest to attempt to pile on her or his lap. Challenging children to find another way will produce wonderful results, among them, everyone getting one big toe on the chair or one child sitting and holding the hand of the nearest child, to whom the rest of the children have linked to form a human chain.

When refining responses, provide feedback that is *neutral but informative.* "I see you're moving across the balance beam on your tummy" or "your three-point balance uses two hands and one foot" is more specific—and less judgmental—than "Good job." The latter doesn't let your students know what about the job was good. It gives no information beyond the fact that you were, for some reason, pleased. Also, when children hear that phrase over and over again, they stop listening to it; the words cease to have meaning. Worse, if you've used that phrase and the job *wasn't* good, your students—who are human lie detectors—will know it isn't true. If you want your students to improve their skills, make sure your comments are both *deserved* and *specific.*

Too often in the past, physical education was taught *to the middle.* Teachers chose activities that could be handled by children of average ability. Although the system may have worked for those children, students who were not as skilled constantly lagged behind, resulting in a vicious cycle of failure that eroded their confidence and led to more failure. Highly skilled children, on the other hand, were not sufficiently challenged and became increasingly bored.

Movement exploration allows *every* child to participate and succeed at his or her own level of development and ability. In addition to the self-confidence and poise continual success brings, this process promotes independence, helps develop patience with oneself and one's peers, and allows the acceptance of others' ideas. Perhaps most important for your students, exploration leads them to the discovery of the richness of possibilities involved in the field of human movement.

Guided Discovery

Because it relies on **convergent problem solving,** which requires a higher level of cognitive ability, guided discovery is most appropriate for students ages five-and-a-half and older who have had considerable experience with problem solving.

With **guided discovery,** you have a specific task or concept in mind, for example, teaching the children to perform a step-hop or that a wide base of support provides the most stable balance. You then lead the children through a sequence of questions and challenges toward discovery of the task. This process, while still allowing for inventiveness and experimentation, guides the children as they *converge* on the right answer.

Although guided discovery takes longer than the direct approach, many educators feel its benefits far outweigh the time factor. When using convergent and divergent problem solving, the children not only learn skills but also learn *how* to learn. Critical-thinking skills are enhanced as the children make choices and decisions (Buschner, 1990). And "most learning takes place when young children are actively engaged in . . . experimenting, experiencing, and raising their own questions and finding answers" (Klein, 1990, p. 27).

Problem solving in general also helps broaden the children's movement vocabulary. Additionally, it reduces fear of failure and thus produces a sense of security that motivates the students to continue experimenting and discovering. Guided discovery, specifically, enables children to find the interconnection of steps within a given task.

❗ TRY THIS

If you want your primary-grade children to learn to execute a step-hop, you could use the direct approach and simply *show* the children how to accomplish it. But that won't excite them much. Instead you can help the children discover it for themselves, which allows them to take ownership of their responses and to develop confidence in their problem-solving abilities. With this approach you might issue the following challenges:

- Practice walking forward and in place with short springy steps.
- Hop in place and then forward, first on one foot and then the other. Change feet often.
- Make up your own combination of walks and hops, using any number of each. Try it first in place and then moving forward.
- Make up a combination of walks and hops that fits into two counts, slightly accenting the first count.

The only correct response to the last challenge is a step-hop because the step is more accented than the hop. Once some students have discovered this, let them demonstrate and ask the rest of the class to try to do it that way. They will then have successfully *discovered* the step-hop.

When using guided discovery with students, it's important to accept all responses—even those considered incorrect. For example, if you've asked a series of questions designed to lead to the execution of a step-hop and some children respond with a skip, which has an uneven instead of even rhythm, you must recognize and validate these responses. Then give the students more time to find another way, or continue asking even more specific questions until they achieve the desired outcome.

It is important that you never provide the answer (Graham, 2001). If you give the answer in the beginning, the discovery process is no longer possible. One can't discover what one already knows. If, following a convergent problem-solving process in which the children don't discover the expected solution, you ultimately give the answer anyway, the students will come to expect this and will be less enthusiastic about exploring possible solutions themselves. Because "wonder and curiosity are valuable mental processes," there is no harm in concluding a lesson in which the children have yet to discover the solution (Graham, 2001, p. 150).

For you, of course, the most difficult part of guided discovery is designing the questions and challenges that will lead students to the desired outcome. Mosston and Ashworth (1990) suggest two techniques for achieving this.

One is to work backward, beginning with the final challenge—the one that will produce the targeted answer. The preceding challenge can then be identified, and so on, back to the first challenge. The second technique is to write a series of commands, as though a direct approach were going to be used. The commands can then be converted to questions.

For example, if you were going to use guided discovery to teach a forward roll, your challenges might include the following:

- Show me an upside-down position with your weight on your hands and feet.

- Show me an upside-down position with your weight on your hands and feet and your tummy facing the floor.

- Show me you can put your bottom way up in the air.

- Look at the ceiling from that position. Try to look at even more of the ceiling.

- Show me you can roll yourself over from that position.

Table 2.1   Advantages and Disadvantages of Teaching Styles

Advantages of the direct style	Disadvantages of the direct style
Uses time efficiently	Doesn't allow for creativity or self-expression
Produces immediate results	Doesn't allow for individual differences in development and skill levels
Teaches children to replicate movements	Focuses on product vs. process
Teaches children to follow directions	
Makes immediate evaluation possible	
Advantages of indirect styles	**Disadvantages of indirect styles**
Enhance critical- and creative-thinking skills	Require more time
Promote self-responsibility	Require practice and patience from teacher
Broaden movement vocabulary	
Lessen fear of failure	
Allow for individual differences	
Develop self-confidence	
Promote independence	
Promote patience with self and peers	
Lead to acceptance of others' ideas	

The goal of the last challenge is a forward roll. Therefore, if you were using the first technique in which you work backward from the desired outcome, you would start with the final challenge and then develop the preceding challenges based on your determination of what would sequentially lead to it. The rationale behind the second technique, in which you pose the challenges as questions, is that you avoid the feeling of a command style of teaching. Still, questions aren't essential. By beginning each challenge with "Show me" or "Let me see you," you avoid sounding like the command style. Also, because the first three challenges can produce divergent responses, this is clearly an indirect, rather than a direct, approach.

Keeping Them Off the Walls

Perhaps the greatest surprise for those who have little or no previous experience with preschoolers and kindergartners is that they just don't *behave* in the way students are expected to behave. Therein lies the crux of the issue: These children may attend school, but their "job description" at this stage of their lives is to be *children*, not students. That means it's unreasonable to expect them to toe the line. Just getting them to *make* a line can be a challenge!

Not to worry, though; common sense plays a big role in keeping the kids from bouncing off the walls and driving you crazy. For example, beginning at the beginning—wherever the children are developmentally—and building from there in a logical progression will ensure that the children are challenged yet not overwhelmed, as will using a problem-solving style of instruction whenever possible. If children are challenged, they won't be bored; if they're not overwhelmed, they won't be frustrated. Boredom and frustration often result in children—of any age—acting out. A child who is experiencing *success* is far less likely to want to wreak havoc on the class.

Still, you have to establish guidelines at the start of the year and practice them just as you would other skills. You also have to enforce them consistently. Setting the stage for expected behavior is a better practice and is less stressful than waiting until students misbehave and then chastising them (Miller, 2000).

Determine what rules you consider most important for your youngest students, and because they're your youngest students, keep the rules to a minimum. Most rules for young children are related to safety. With that in mind, you have to determine what guidelines are needed to keep the students safe (e.g., no participating in stocking feet, no gum allowed). Beyond that, however, you want to implement guidelines that create the greatest potential for success and the least amount of frustration for your students and you.

Guidelines

One essential protocol is *We will respect one another's personal space.* At first, this may be difficult to enforce because young children generally enjoy bumping into each other. So it's your challenge to make the children *want* to avoid colliding or interfering with one another. Start by exploring the concept of personal space while the children are stationary. Ideas for doing so are described in the next chapter. Then, when the children are moving, use the image of each child being inside a giant bubble, also described in the next chapter. They should stay far enough away from one another to avoid bursting anyone's bubble (see figure 2.5).

Figure 2.5   Using the image of being surrounded by giant bubbles can help children grasp the concept of personal space—their own and others'.

Of course, children being children, they just may *enjoy* bursting one another's bubbles. Should that be the case, use the image of dolphins swimming. Children who've seen these creatures in action, either at an aquarium or on television, will be able to relate to the fact that dolphins move side by side but never get close enough to touch one another. The goal, then, is for your students to behave similarly.

A second essential protocol is *We will participate with as little noise as possible.* Naturally, you can't expect silence. But you shouldn't have to raise your voice or shout to have your challenges, directions, and follow-up questions heard. One way to avoid this is to establish an auditory or visual signal indicating it's time to stop, look, and listen: Stop, look at me, and listen for what comes next. Choose a signal the students have to watch for (two fingers held in the air or the time-out sign from sports) or something they must listen for (a hand clap, a strike on a triangle, or two taps on a drum) and make it their secret code. Little ones love such things.

With some classes, either possibility works well. With more challenging groups of children, you'll probably find an audible signal more effective than a visual one. After all, children can avoid looking if they want to, but they can't avoid hearing. If you choose an audible signal, however, be aware that your voice isn't the best choice because the children hear it so often. Also, your signal should be a quiet one that can't be heard above a lot of noise, which rules out a whistle.

Whatever your signal, it is reasonable to expect the children to stop, look, and listen within four seconds of seeing or hearing it. And you should have to give the signal only once (Graham, 2001). This, however, will take practice, sometimes considerable practice.

Young children are generally willing to follow rules as long as they know what's expected of them, there aren't a *lot* of rules, and the rules have some significance for them. With that in mind, you shouldn't simply tell your students what the rules are; you should tell them why they're necessary.

Following, in no particular order, are other teaching tips to help you keep students focused and on the ground.

Establish Boundaries

Too much space, as in a large gym, can be overwhelming to some children. You also don't want them roaming so far from you and the group that they're either unable to hear you or no longer seem to be part of the activity. Use masking tape, rope, or plastic cones to outline the boundaries.

Use Positive Challenges

If you assume the students are capable of handling your challenges, they're more likely to *be* capable. For example, "Find two ways to . . ." assumes students can find ways to respond. Similarly, "Show me you can . . ." implies you *know* they can. Conversely, if you present challenges by asking, "Can you . . . ?" you're implying a choice, and many young children will simply say no.

Also, young children love to show off, especially for their teachers. Therefore, if you introduce challenges with phrases like "Show me you can" or "Let me see you," the children will *want* to show you they can. Positive challenges are a simple technique but amazingly effective.

Use Your Voice as a Tool

This is a straightforward, commonsense suggestion. If you want the children to move slowly, *speak* slowly. If you want them to move quietly, *speak* quietly. Also, just as you can catch more flies with honey than vinegar, you can attract and maintain more attention with a lower volume than with a higher one. Children are far more likely to react positively to a whisper than to a yell.

Monitor Energy Levels

Movement activities can generate an abundance of energy, and too much energy can result in frustrating, unproductive, unmanageable classes. Too little energy can have comparable results because tired children tend to display irritability and off-task behavior.

If you find that the children as a whole have too little energy, use lively music to inspire them. If they're overexcited, put on a piece of soothing music. Usually, *alternating* vigorous and quieter activities is enough to ensure against frenzy and fatigue. For example, if the children have been performing gross motor movement, you could follow up with nonlocomotor movement or even a relaxation exercise. An example of the latter is an activity called I'm Melting! in which you invite students to demonstrate what it would look like to melt, as though they were snow or ice sculptures, ice cream cones, or the witch in *The Wizard of Oz*.

However, if the children have an excess of energy (which is more often the case) and nothing you try works to rein them in, sit and watch them run! They'll be practicing a locomotor skill, promoting cardiorespiratory endurance, and having fun. What more could you ask from a lesson? And when they've burned themselves out, they'll come back to you out of breath and ready to do whatever you ask.

Nonparticipants and Disruptive Students

You're likely to encounter two specific problems, and regardless of your policies when you encounter them in older students, you'll once again have to handle things differently with the little ones. The first is the nonparticipant, and the other is the disruptive child. We'll address them one at a time.

Nonparticipants

Sometimes, especially at the beginning of the school year, some children don't want to participate. There are several reasons for this, and your first step is to determine their reasons, initially eliminating physical problems as the cause. Although it's sad, some children refuse to take part out of a fear of looking foolish or being wrong. That may surprise you in children so young, but this fear is already instilled in many preschoolers and is quite powerful.

For these children, observing success-oriented movement experiences is often the key to unlocking their fear. They'll notice, for example, that 20 of their classmates have responded to your challenges in 20 different ways, and you're validating all the responses. They'll begin to realize that there's no right or wrong, and with a bit of gentle coaxing and positive reinforcement, you can eventually encourage these children to join in.

Some children are genuinely shy and only need time to get used to the idea of moving with the rest of the group, while others will require specific encouragement from you or another adult. Sometimes merely standing near the shy child as you lead movement activities, offering occasional smiles or gentle touches, is the only encouragement you need to offer. At other times, positive reinforcement of any level of participation will do much to contribute to the shy child's confidence. For example, if you've asked the children to freeze and the nonparticipant is sitting particularly still, use her as an example of stillness. If you've asked the children to move just one body part and the nonparticipant smiles, acknowledge his response. Be aware, however, that some children use nonparticipation as a way of getting adult attention. You can generally tell that this is the case if the student seems to thrive on your attention, or if any attention you provide results in disruptive behavior. If that's the case, ignoring all nonparticipation is your best strategy.

Whatever the reason for the lack of involvement and no matter what your policy is with older children, young children shouldn't be forced to join in. This can place undue emotional stress on them, which can create an extreme dislike for physical activity. However, you can insist that they are not allowed to do anything else, that they take on the role of audience, sometimes even giving them something specific to watch for. Not only does this involve them to a certain extent, but it also ensures that they're gaining something from the experience, because children can absorb much from watching movement. Occasionally, you may even be pleasantly surprised to learn from a parent that a child who merely watches from the sidelines imitates everything she sees in the privacy of her own home.

Disruptive Students

Disruptive behavior tends to be a more significant problem than nonparticipation. Because even negative attention is better than none at all, many children use disruptive behavior as a way to receive attention from adults. Unfortunately, because disruptions are annoying, distracting, and sometimes dangerous, children causing them often get more attention than those who are behaving well. But you should never let a class fall apart in order to respond to one child. That's why ignoring the behavior is often the most effective policy. Because the child doesn't receive the attention he's seeking, there is no need to continue the behavior.

Of course, ignoring may be the best policy when the behavior is just annoying or mildly distracting. But if it's harmful to the child or others, it has to be stopped immediately. Sometimes you can redirect the child's focus elsewhere. For instance, a child making noise stamping her feet can be asked to demonstrate tiptoeing or other substitutes for stamping. If that doesn't work, a single warning, issued firmly but gently, is often enough to end the behavior. Undivided attention involving eye contact, a body position at the child's level, appropriate touch, and use of the child's name is far more effective than yelling from a distance (Miller, 2000).

Should all of this fail and the harmful behavior continues, remove the child from the group calmly and without anger to allow for a cooling-off period for the child and for you. Philosophies regarding time-out specifics vary. One suggestion is continuing the time-out until the child comes to you and explains why he was asked to sit out (Graham, Holt/Hale, and Parker, 2003). Another is questioning the child about the reason for the isolation and how it can be prevented in the future (Gallahue, 1993). Still another philosophy contends that the child knows the reason and no further discussion is necessary (Essa, 2007). The length of a time-out is also a matter of philosophy. Some recommend a time-out lasting the remainder of the class should a child misbehave a second time; others believe that exclusion for longer than five minutes is less effective than shorter periods (Graham et al., 2003; French, Silliman, and Henderson, 1990). Also, some children use disruptive behavior to get out of class; thus, a time-out gives them exactly what they want.

How you handle time-outs has to be a personal choice. Experts generally agree, however, that once a child is asked to sit out, he should be ignored. Also, a time-out must be used *sparingly,* or it becomes an ineffective management technique.

REMEMBER THIS

Chances are, regardless of how many tips and techniques you have in your repertoire, there will be days when you wonder why you didn't choose a different profession. But if you understand that kids in early childhood are a whole different "breed of animal" and you maintain your sense of humor, those days will occur less often than the ones on which you experience satisfaction at a job well done.

- For young children, physical education begins with body-part identification. It isn't until age seven that most know their large and small body parts.

- Body-part activities are often stationary, but they make wonderful warm-up or cool-down activities. They can also provide practice with nonlocomotor skills, promote flexibility, and develop an awareness of the levels in space.

- The direct approach is the teaching style most appropriate for activities in which all the children must perform in exactly the same way, as when playing Follow the Leader.
- Immediate results and the efficient use of time are the most significant advantages of the direct approach.
- The direct approach doesn't allow for individual differences in development and skill level, which is a significant disadvantage.
- Movement exploration—also known as divergent problem solving—allows for a variety of responses to a single challenge and should be your most-used teaching method with the little ones.
- Guided discovery—also known as convergent problem solving—requires a higher level of cognitive ability and is therefore most appropriate for the older, more experienced of your little ones.
- Feedback should be neutral and informative.
- Children experiencing success are less likely to want to wreak havoc on your class.
- You must establish protocols at the beginning of the year, practice them, and enforce them consistently.

3

Elements
of Movement

Critical to any program of movement education—and certainly to early childhood physical education—is the concept of movement *variations*. Exploring movement variations allows children to discover the unlimited possibilities for performing locomotor, nonlocomotor, manipulative, dance, and gymnastic skills. Students are able to fully experience each movement. Most important, exploring movement variations makes a significant contribution to the body and spatial awareness that are the foundation of what it means to be physically educated. As a bonus, exploring movement variations promotes children's creativity and problem-solving skills.

Movement variations are achieved through the use of the **elements of movement,** sometimes called movement concepts. These are space, shape, time, force, flow, and rhythm. For instance, if the locomotor skill of walking were being explored, there would be several choices for *how* to perform the walk: forward, backward, to the side, or possibly in a circle, in which the element of *space* is being used. The walk could be performed with arms or head held in various positions (*shape*), quickly or slowly (*time*), strongly or lightly (*force*), with interruptions (*flow*), or to altering beats (*rhythm*).

If we liken movement education to the study of grammar, the skills themselves can be considered *verbs,* and the elements of space, shape, time, force, flow, and rhythm are the *adverbs* modifying them (see figure 3.1).

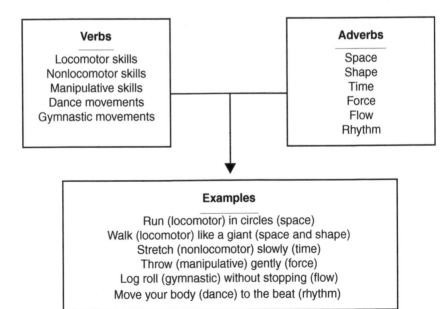

Figure 3.1 Movement as grammar.

Although the study of grammar typically teaches verbs first, your program should initially focus on the adverbs—the elements of movement—because young children initially experience more success with them than with the mature execution of motor skills. Also, exploring the elements of movement helps teach children to better execute motor skills. Finally, understanding and using them promotes learning in all three domains of development.

Each of the six elements of movement, listed in a general progression from least to most challenging, is described in more detail.

Space

The element of space is divided into two components. The first, **personal space,** is the area immediately surrounding the body and includes whatever can be reached while a person remains in one spot. It can be likened to a large bubble surrounding the body. The rest is referred to as **general space** (or *shared space*) and is limited only by the location in which you're working. In a gym, the general space is typically defined by the floors, walls, and ceilings.

Both general and personal space have three levels. When standing upright, the child is at the middle level. Anything closer to the ground is considered the low level. Positions or movements performed on tiptoe or in the air occur at the high level.

Space also involves the bodily and spatial directions of forward and backward and right and left. Finally, movement performed through general space entails pathways: straight, curving, or zigzagging.

It's important to begin your program with an exploration (or, in the case of returning classes, a reinforcement) of the concept of space, particularly personal space. Stationary body-part activities like Head, Belly, Toes (see page 13) give your young students initial experience with personal space and with the three levels in space. But if you want your students to be able to move through general space without interfering with others or, worse, harming themselves or others, body-part activities alone aren't enough. This is particularly true for the many young children who have little or no sense of their own personal space. You'll recognize these children because they're the ones bumping into everyone and everything, or who line up too close to other children.

To explore personal space, play Inside My Bubble. Provide the children carpet squares, hoops, or poly spots, and ask them to imagine that when they're standing on or inside one of these items, they're each inside their own giant bubble. Ask students to imagine that they're holding a paintbrush, then invite them to "paint" the inside of their bubbles without stepping off the carpet square or poly spot or out of the hoop. Explain that what they're creating is their own personal space.

This simple activity requires the children to consider the extent of the space immediately surrounding them. It has the added bonus of granting them ownership of that space because it's something they've "created" themselves. That means that they'll be more likely to want to preserve it and that they'll be more inclined to respect the personal space of others. In other words, it gives them less incentive to want to "crash and go boom."

Once the children have painted their bubbles, present challenges such as the following:

- Show me how low you can get inside your bubble.
- Stay very low, and move your arms all around your bubble in as many ways as you can think of.
- Show me how high up you can get while staying inside your bubble. Find a way to get very high with your feet still on the floor. Now find a way with your feet coming off the floor.
- Move your body so it's between very high and very low. Move your arms in as many ways as possible all around your body.
- Move your feet so they're far apart but still inside your bubble. Show me how wide you can make your whole body while still inside your bubble.

An excellent way to help children understand that they take their personal space with them wherever they go is to give each student a hoop to pick up and hold around his or her waist. Explain to the students that the hoop represents their personal space, or bubble, and invite them to walk around the room without letting their hoop touch anyone else's. If you don't have hoops, or enough hoops, perform this and the next activity with the children extending their arms out to their sides. Encourage students to make straight, curving, and zigzagging paths. Once they've had ample time to experiment with a forward direction, ask them to try to keep from touching one another while moving backward (the back of the body going first). Finally, invite them to try moving sideways, leading with one and then the other side of the body.

Once the children have achieved success with these challenges, make the activity a bit more difficult by playing a game called Shrinking Room (see figure 3.2). The children perform the same actions just described, but this time you act as a moveable wall by standing with your arms out to your sides. Begin at one end of the room, allowing the children the greatest amount of space in which to move. Every couple of minutes, however, take a step or two forward, thereby shrinking the space available. Despite the increasingly limited space, the goal is for the children to continue to move without touching anyone else's hoop. Always stop while the children are still able to experience success.

Figure 3.2   Playing Shrinking Room helps children understand both personal and general space.

When they're exploring general space, of course, the children will have to execute locomotor skills; they can't move in different directions and along different pathways without walking, running, or performing some other traveling skill. With your youngest students, however, you'll first want to emphasize their understanding of personal and general space

 TRY THIS

With children ages six through eight you can use imagery related to astronauts to get across the idea of both personal and general space. Ask the students to find their personal space and to get into the smallest shape possible on the floor. They then imagine that they're astronauts, each in his or her space capsule, and that they have landed on an unknown planet. At your signal they begin exploring, with either their arms or legs, all of the area immediately surrounding their capsules. They continue this process, slowly rising. Once they've explored all the area they can reach from within their capsules, they venture out onto the "planet" so they can report on it when they return to Earth. At your signal, they begin reversing the process, finally ending up once again enclosed in their own capsules.

before concentrating on how well they're executing the locomotor skill. For example, if you've challenged them to gallop in zigzagging pathways, your first concern will be whether or not they can create zigzagging pathways. Naturally, you can take note of students who seem to have difficulty galloping, but focus on helping them improve their galloping skills at a later point in the program.

Shape

The study of **shape** relates to the various forms the body is capable of assuming. This element is sometimes referred to as the relationship of body parts because whenever the relationship between or among body parts changes, so does the body's shape. For example, if a hand is brought closer to a foot, the body bends and the spine curves. If that hand is taken as far from the foot as possible, the body must straighten, and a new body shape results.

An excellent introduction to the element of shape is to play the Mirror Game. Stand facing the students, who are scattered throughout the room, each in his or her own personal space, meaning there is enough room between them to extend their arms without touching anyone else. Start moving slowly to create different body shapes. The students, who are pretending to be your mirror reflection, replicate each shape. When the children are ready for the responsibility of working in partners, they can play this game in pairs; each partner takes a turn leading.

To further explore shape and to offer the children additional experience with personal space, present challenges such as the following:

- Show me how round you can be.
- Show me how flat (wide, narrow, long, short, crooked, straight) you can make your body.
- Show me you can look like a chair (a table).
- Show me you can look like a ball (pencil, flower, teapot, rug).

Of course, you should also challenge the children to experiment with the shapes they can make with their bodies while performing locomotor skills, which are described in more detail in the next chapter. For instance, while exploring walking, invite the children to walk holding their arms in different positions (e.g., on hips, overhead, out to the sides, or as though they are very big or very small). The first example offers experience with finding the body's center of gravity and the second with the concept of levels. Also, because *big* and *small* are both adjectives and quantitative concepts, the activity falls under the content areas of language arts and mathematics.

Time

The element of **time** relates to how slowly or quickly a movement is performed. Movement, however, is not only slow or fast but also includes the range of speed in between. With young children, it's best to introduce this element by contrasting the extremes of slow and fast before exploring the continuum from one to the other.

Music is a wonderful tool in helping to make the concepts of slow and fast less abstract to children (see figure 3.3). Play a slow piece of music and suggest ways in which the students can accompany it, for example, by pretending to move through peanut butter or to be in slow-motion instant replay. Then contrast this by playing a piece of music with a fast tempo and inviting them to move, for instance, like bumblebees (Rimsky-Korsakov's "Flight of the Bumblebee" is great for this), a mouse running from a cat, or a movie in fast-forward, depending on what feels most appropriate to the music.

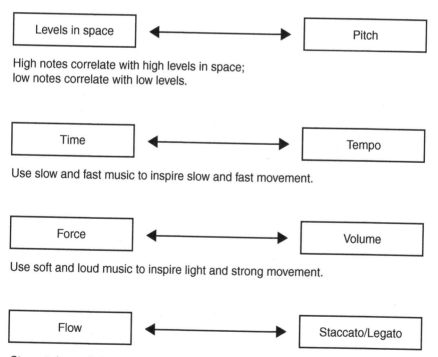

| Levels in space | ⟷ | Pitch |

High notes correlate with high levels in space;
low notes correlate with low levels.

| Time | ⟷ | Tempo |

Use slow and fast music to inspire slow and fast movement.

| Force | ⟷ | Volume |

Use soft and loud music to inspire light and strong movement.

| Flow | ⟷ | Staccato/Legato |

Staccato is music in which the notes are punctuated, like bound flow.
Legato indicates the music is played without any noticeable interruptions.
The music flows smoothly, like free flow in movement.

Figure 3.3   Connections between movement and musical elements.

This combination of music and imagery is powerful for children, but it's also possible to use imagery alone. If you do so, you'll stimulate their imaginations and thus their creativity. But if you want to elicit the appropriate responses from them (or any response at all), you'll have to use only images to which the children can relate, either through personal experience or through television or movies. Melting ice cream, for instance, will be more familiar to them than a moving glacier. A bumblebee will typically be more familiar than a hummingbird. Other images that lend themselves to the element of time include the movements of a turtle, a snail or worm, a broken-down car, and a stalking cat for slow and a racecar, jet plane, or speed boat for fast.

When your students demonstrate that they understand the extremes of slow and fast and are able to perform at those speeds, introduce them to the continuum from one to the other. For example, you might lead them, in follow-the-leader fashion, slowly around the gym, *gradually* increasing your pace. When you're going as fast as you want to go, gradually decrease your tempo, bringing them back to the original pace.

! TRY THIS

Slow movement requires much more control than fast movement and simply isn't as much fun for children, so you'll have to give them fun reasons to do it! One slow activity students enjoy is Slo-Mo, in which they act out something from sports or a movie that's being shown in slow motion.

"Beep Beep" is a song from the 1950s, performed by the Playmates, that is an example of *accelerando,* the gradual increase in tempo. It's great fun to perform follow-the-leader style, gradually increasing the pace of your movements along with the tempo of the music. It starts out very slowly and ends up *really* fast, and because it's so silly, the kids love it. (It's a wonderful cardiovascular activity.) You can find this song on several Web sites; just enter "Beep Beep Playmates" into your search engine.

Force

Force concerns how strongly or lightly a movement is performed and the amount of muscle tension involved. Tiptoeing, for instance, requires much less force and muscle tension than does stamping the feet. Similarly, moving like a butterfly requires much less force than moving like a dinosaur. With this element, too, it's best to contrast the extremes before exploring the continuum from one to the other.

To introduce students to the element of force, invite them to play Statues and Rag Dolls, in which they alternately pretend to be a statue and then a rag doll. Point out that the former uses muscles that feel tight, while the latter feels loose. This is also an excellent cool-down exercise because contracting and releasing the muscles promotes relaxation. Always end with the rag doll. Other challenges that will familiarize your students with force include the following:

- Make strong movements with your arms, like the propellers on a helicopter.
- Make very light arm movements, like a butterfly's wings.
- Stomp your feet across the floor.
- Tiptoe across the floor.
- Move like a toy soldier.
- Move very softly, like a snowflake or a feather floating.
- Pretend to be a robot.
- Show me an astronaut floating weightlessly in outer space.

Music is an excellent tool to use with this element as well. Moving to soft music tends to inspire gentle movement, while moving to loud music inspires the opposite.

Once children have grasped the concepts of light and strong movements, introduce them to the continuum from one to the other in a follow-the-leader activity (Exploring Force), as you did with the element of time. Here, though, you begin by tiptoeing, gradually increasing the weight of your steps until you're stamping forcefully. You can then reverse the process.

Flow

The **flow** of movement is either bound or free. Bound flow is punctuated, or interrupted, and free flow is uninterrupted. If we liken it to a sentence, bound flow is one in which there are commas and periods. Free flow is like a sentence in which there may be a breathing pause but not a complete pause until the period at the end. In movement terms, bound flow is exemplified in the motion of a mechanical toy, or a series requiring the children to hop-hop-stop, hop-hop-stop. Free flow is demonstrated when the children pretend to be skaters gliding effortlessly across the ice or eagles soaring.

Introduce the element of flow to your students with a game of Statues, in which they move in any way they want while music is playing and freeze into statues when the music stops (you press the pause button). To explore this element without music, ask the children to move freely around the room until they hear your signal to freeze. As soon as they hear it, they must stop and not move another muscle until they hear your signal to go again. Vary the time between signals, sometimes letting the children experience periods of free flow and sometimes interrupting frequently.

Rhythm

Rhythm, although often associated with the element of time, is cited as a separate element because of its many facets and benefits to students. This element not only relates to music but also encompasses the many rhythms of life. Words, for instance, have rhythm, as do the various locomotor skills (e.g., the rhythm of a hop is different from that of a gallop). People, in fact, possess their own personal rhythms for both thinking and functioning. For example, when you ask the children to get into a small shape, each will respond at his or her own pace.

Clapping activities can demonstrate the rhythm of words. Sit in a circle with the children. Then, saying your name aloud, clap one clap per syllable. (Rae Pica, pronounced Ray Pee-ka, would involve three claps with a pause between the first and second.) Now ask the children to do it with you. Go around the circle, saying and clapping the rhythm of each child's name. Use the first name or first and last, depending on the developmental level of your group. This is not only a good introduction to rhythm, but it also makes a great warm-up activity, particularly at the beginning of the school year when you and the children are learning each other's names.

To explore the various rhythms of locomotor skills, as the children are performing a skill, begin to beat a drum or clap your hands to the rhythm of their movement. It will be a while before the children will be able to match a rhythm you impose on them, so you can't yet clap your hands or beat a drum and expect them to move in time to the beats; but you can match theirs. This allows the children to concurrently *hear, see,* and *feel* the different rhythms, and the more senses used in the learning process, the more children retain (Fauth, 1990).

Music is valuable here as well. If you expose the children to a variety of musical styles, cultures, and time periods, you'll automatically expose them to a variety of rhythms. When they begin to feel comfortable moving to various rhythms, they'll be on their way to a future in which they feel comfortable with their bodies and confident in their movement skills.

➡ REMEMBER THIS

When you use the elements of movement to vary the students' responses, you give them an opportunity to more fully experience the possibilities for each movement, thus broadening their movement vocabularies, offering them more opportunities to experience success, and expanding the possibility that physical activity, in one form or another, will become a part of your students' later lives.

- Exploring movement variations makes a significant contribution to body and spatial awareness, which are the foundation of a physical education program.
- The movement skills themselves can be considered the verbs of your program, and the movement elements are the adverbs that modify them.
- Focus first on your students' use of the movement elements before emphasizing correct execution of the movement skills.
- Music is a wonderful tool in helping to make concepts such as *slow, fast, light,* and *heavy* less abstract to children.
- You'll generate the greatest response from children if you use imagery to which young children can relate.

4

Fundamental Motor Skill Development

I t makes sense for students to acquire fundamental skills before trying to tackle skills that are more complex. After all, you wouldn't expect them to try diving before they knew how to swim. Similarly, if they were new to skiing, it would be a lot wiser for them to conquer the bunny slopes before heading to Devil's Peak.

In the same way, it's unrealistic to expect young children to catch a small white ball when capturing a 12-inch (30-centimeter) playground ball is still not a sure thing. It's unrealistic to want young children to simultaneously run and kick before being able to do either of these things well on its own. Similarly, it makes little sense to ask young children to walk a balance beam before they're walking the *floor* with correct posture and form.

Asking children to attain unrealistic goals—to perform skills they have little hope of doing well, let alone mastering—is, as they say, putting the cart before the horse. The result is often frustration and failure, which in turn can lead to a distaste for physical activity in general. And that's certainly not what you want to teach them.

This chapter looks at the ABCs of movement, enabling you to put the horse before the cart. By facilitating learning of the fundamentals first, you'll help your young students feel competent and confident in their movement abilities, ensuring they'll later be physically and emotionally ready to tackle more challenging tasks.

Acquiring Motor Skills

Motor skills can be broken down into two general types: fine motor skills and gross motor skills. **Fine motor skills** are those that involve movement of the small muscles controlling the hands, fingers, and thumbs in coordination with the eyes. Children who are learning to write or play an instrument would be developing their fine motor skills. **Gross motor skills** involve movement using the large muscles of the body. Children practicing any of the locomotor skills (running, leaping, and so on) would be developing gross motor skills.

Many people believe children automatically acquire motor skills as their bodies develop, that it's a natural, "magical" process that occurs along with maturation. Unfortunately, this is an easy assumption to make. After all, one day the infant rolls over by herself, eventually starts to crawl, and then suddenly rises up onto hands and knees and begins creeping. Somewhere around her first birthday, with only a little assistance and a lot of enthusiasm from adults, she takes her first steps. And then it seems, almost before anyone realizes it's happening, she's off and running.

So it certainly appears that motor skills miraculously occur and pretty much take care of themselves. And, to a certain extent, it's true. However, maturation takes care of only part of the process, the part that allows a child to execute most movement skills at an immature level. Thus, many children never achieve mature patterns for many motor skills. As evidence of this, an Australian study of 1,200 students between the ages of 5 and 12 found an "appalling" level of ability in basic motor skills (Colman, 1996). The following are among the findings:

- The 11-year-old boys were best able to perform a vertical jump, but only 11 percent of them could do it properly.
- Only about 45 percent of elementary school students could catch with correct form.
- Only two to three percent of the 12-year-olds could hit a softball or baseball correctly.
- Fewer than 10 percent of the children were able to run correctly.

It's evident, therefore, that just as reading and writing must be taught in early childhood, so, too, must motor skills. And that begins with the basic locomotor and nonlocomotor skills, *each skill* progressing through stages of development.

Learning to ride a bicycle is a great example of the process involved in acquiring a new motor skill (Kirchner, 2001). If you think back, you'll probably recall how unsteady your initial attempts were and how much concentration the effort required. Gradually you became more proficient at keeping the bike upright. But stopping and turning—different skills entirely—still required effort and concentration.

Similarly, when a child first learns to walk, it takes tremendous effort and concentration just to remain erect. With practice, gravity is overcome, but the baby still requires a wide stance to feel secure. With more practice, the child's position improves until the feet are moving side by side, arms swinging in opposition, with upright posture and weight distributed evenly over all five toes, which are pointed straight ahead. The motion becomes automatic and efficient. This, at least, is the goal, and it's a process that takes considerable time. When the child begins to run, however, he won't automatically achieve a mature form simply because he's able to walk well. Because running is a much more demanding skill, gravity will once again prove to be a challenge, as will posture and coordination.

Different physical education texts use different terms to describe the process involved in moving through these stages. Kirchner labels the stages *initial, intermediate,* and *automatic.* The first, as he describes it, involves as much thinking about a skill as trying to perform it. The intermediate phase represents a gradual shift from acquiring the fundamentals of the skill to a more focused effort to refine it. In the final phase, the skill feels and looks automatic.

Gallahue (1993) describes essentially the same three phases of motor learning and labels them the *initial stage*, the *elementary stage*, and the *mature stage*. And Graham, Holt/Hale, and Parker (2003) have chosen four categories to describe what they call generic levels of skill proficiency. The first, the *precontrol* level, represents the stage at which a child is unable to either consciously control or intentionally replicate a movement. They use the example of a child's initial attempts to bounce a ball, during which the child spends more time chasing it than bouncing it. The ball, rather than the child, seems to be in control. At the *control* (advanced beginner) level, the movement is much closer to the child's actual intentions, although a good deal of concentration is still required. When children reach the *utilization* level in a particular skill, they don't have to think as much about how to execute the skill and are able to use it in different contexts, such as in a game. The *proficiency* level is the advanced stage and represents the level at which a movement appears effortless and an individual is able to use it in changing environments and repeat it with ever-increasing degrees of quality.

For each new skill learned, a child will begin at, adopting the terminology of Graham and colleagues, the precontrol level. Then, depending on the skill involved, it can be a long time before children move through the control level and on to the utilization level, ready to actually *use* the skill in a situation as dynamic and unpredictable as a game.

Motor development, therefore, may be age related, but it is not age dependent. A child isn't automatically at the utilization level simply because he's eight years old. Nor would it be correct to assume that all middle schoolers, for example, are adept at all the basic motor skills and are ready to take them to the next level just because they're 11 or 12.

Age alone is not an agent of change (Sayre and Gallagher, 2001). Age merely marks a passage of time. It's what *happens* during that passage of

❓ CONSIDER THIS

A child moves from an immature level of skill development to a higher level in the same way one gets to Carnegie Hall: practice, practice, practice. According to the American Academy of Pediatrics (1992, p. 1002), "During the preschool years, motor skills are best learned in an unstructured, noncompetitive setting in which a child can experiment and learn by trial and error on an individual basis. Specific skills can be refined through repetitive practice only after the relevant level of motor development has been reached."

time that determines a child's readiness to move on to the next level of development. And what happens during that passage of time should be considerable instruction and practice.

Despite a reluctance to assign ages or grades to the various stages of skill development, the experts do agree that elementary aged students never reach the proficiency level for most motor skills. And it's probably not unrealistic to say that you should be satisfied with helping your pre-schoolers and kindergartners advance from precontrol to control levels. With your first- and second-graders, you can set a goal of reaching the utilization level for most basic motor skills.

Skills

Following are descriptions of the locomotor and nonlocomotor skills that comprise the fundamentals that should form the foundation of children's early PE experiences. Also included are numerous suggestions for exploring them with your students. Figure 4.1 lists the locomotor and nonlocomotor skills, each in a general developmental progression from bottom to top.

Locomotor Skills

Sometimes called *traveling skills,* **locomotor skills** transport the body as a whole from one point to another. Children acquire the ability to execute locomotor skills according to their own internal timetables. The following represents a general developmental progression of locomotor skills. Each skill is defined here, accompanied by sample activities.

Crawl

The crawl involves lying on the belly, with head and shoulders raised off the floor and the weight of the upper torso supported by the elbows (see figure 4.2a). Locomotion involves moving the elbows and hips. Children should explore homolateral crawling (simultaneously moving the arm and leg on the same side of the body) as well as cross-lateral crawling (moving the limbs in opposition—e.g., left arm and right leg together).

You may think that your students are too old to explore such a simple motor skill, but it is cross-lateral movement that activates both hemispheres of the brain and promotes communication across the corpus callosum, the matter between the two hemispheres. Children who have experienced too little cross-lateral activity are often unable to cross the midline of the body and can eventually experience difficulties with reading and writing (Hannaford, 2005).

To make crawling fun and less "babyish," invite the children to pretend to be worms, seals, or snakes. Eventually you can challenge partners to

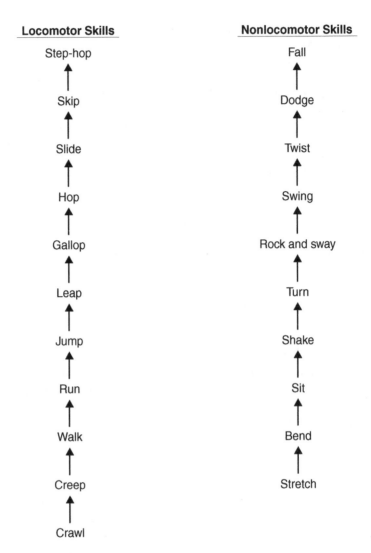

Figure 4.1   Categories of motor skills.

be longer snakes, made possible by one child holding onto the ankles of a child in front of her. The ultimate challenge is for the children to continue joining together until they've created one very long snake.

Creep

This skill requires using the hands and knees or hands and feet to move the body through space (see figure 4.2*b*). It is the child's first *efficient* form of locomotion and what parents usually refer to as *crawling*. Because it

Figure 4.2 Examples of locomotor skills: *(a)* Crawling occurs on the tummy; *(b)* creeping is performed on "all fours."

is also a cross-lateral activity, children, especially those who haven't yet achieved a mature level of cross-pattern creeping, should be given ample opportunity to practice, even in the early elementary years.

The children can pretend to be the following creatures that creep: dogs, cats, spiders, babies, turtles, and crabs. Talk to your students about the differences among these creatures and how each moves. Then invite them to pretend to be each of them, one at a time.

Walk

The walk moves the body through space by transferring weight from the ball and toes of one foot to the heel of the other. Continual contact is made with the floor. Limbs are used in opposition.

By the time children are six, they can usually walk with a mature pattern. However, posture and foot alignment should be monitored. The body must be kept straight and toes pointed straight ahead, with the weight evenly

CONSIDER THIS

Since 1992, when the American Academy of Pediatrics introduced its "Back to Sleep" campaign, encouraging parents to put their infants to sleep on their backs (to reduce the incidence of sudden infant death syndrome), babies have spent less time on their tummies. Many, uncomfortable with the position, skip the creeping stage altogether. But babies who do so often lack upper-torso, shoulder, and neck strength and may have trouble with bilateral coordination, crossing the midline, and visual tracking, among other problems. Therefore, any creeping or cross-lateral activities you do with your students will contribute to their development in numerous ways.

Hannaford (2005) tells the story of Todd, a 16-year-old high school student who wasn't able to read, despite significant amounts of time, energy, and money spent. Then, one weekend, his mother discovered Brain Gym, a program developed by Paul Dennison to strengthen the mind–body connection. She introduced Todd to the cross-crawl, a standing movement in which he alternated touching an elbow to the opposite knee, and thus crossed his body's midline. To ensure that Todd would practice this movement, the whole family cross-crawled before he went to school in the morning and before he went to bed at night. In just *six weeks* Todd was reading—at grade level! Hannaford explains that he had all the information he needed stored in the two hemispheres of his brain; it just wasn't communicating across the corpus callosum, the matter connecting the hemispheres. Performing the cross-crawl required the hemispheres to communicate across the corpus callosum.

distributed over all five toes. Rolling the foot in so that the small toes lift off the ground, known as pronating, is a common problem.

To make walking fun, use emotional imagery: walking as though mad, scared, sad, big and strong (confident), or proud. You can also use the imagery of different environments: walking as though on hot sand that's burning the feet, in a dense jungle, or in a haunted house, or trying to get through sticky mud or deep snow. Remember to keep the children's ages and experiences in mind when choosing imagery.

Run

Running transfers the body's weight from the ball and toes of one foot to the ball and toes of the other. The body should be inclined slightly forward, and the arms should be slightly bent, swinging in opposition to the legs.

Running is one of the most demanding activities, requiring "much of the heart, lungs, and muscles. For the young child it also makes demands on the nervous system for all parts of the body must be used alternately, symmetrically, and yet with synchronous timing; contraction and relaxation must alternate smoothly; an even rhythm must be maintained; balance makes new demands as strides lengthen and ground is covered rapidly" (Sinclair, 1973, p. 23).

To explore running with imagery, ask the children to run as though crossing hot sand, finishing a long race, playing basketball, trying to catch a bus, and trying to score a touchdown. You can also encourage them to pretend they're in an imaginary track meet, maybe at the Olympics. Accompanying the activity with a piece of music in an even 4/4 meter and a tempo appropriate for running can add to the activity. The theme from the movie *Chariots of Fire* is perfect.

Jump

A jump propels the body upward from a takeoff on one or both feet. The toes, which are the last part of the foot to leave the ground (heel-ball-toe) are the first to reach it on landing; landing occurs on both feet (toe-ball-heel). Knees should bend to absorb the shock of landing.

As mentioned earlier, an Australian study discovered that only 11 percent of the 11-year-old boys involved were able to correctly perform a vertical jump (Colman, 1996). Common errors among young children are failing to land with knees bent and failing to land with the heels coming all the way to the floor. Because jumping is integral to many sports and physical activities, it's important to correct errors such as these early.

Having something to jump *over* makes practicing this skill fun for young children. Begin with a single jump rope stretched out on the floor, and ask the students to jump back and forth across it. Then progress to laying two jump ropes parallel to each other, at first only a couple of inches apart and gradually increasing the distance between them. Children also enjoy jumping in and out of a hoop lying flat on the floor.

To employ imagery, invite students to jump as though they were rabbits, kangaroos, bouncing balls, or frogs. They can also pretend to be reaching for something high above them, to be having a temper tantrum, or to be startled by a loud noise. Finally, ask them to show you how they jump for joy.

Leap

The leap is similar to a run, except that the knee and ankle action is greater (see figure 4.3). The knee leads forward following the takeoff and is then extended as the foot reaches forward to land. The back leg extends to the rear while in the air, but once the front foot has landed, the rear leg swings forward into the next lift. Leaps are often combined with running

Figure 4.3 A student leaps from one poly spot to another.

steps to achieve greater height and distance.

Preschoolers often best relate to this motor skill through imagery or with a prop. To use imagery, you can ask them to pretend to leap over a puddle, a hurdle (like in a track meet), a tall building (like Superman), or a fallen log in the woods (like a deer). Props might include a rope held an inch or two (2.5 to 5 centimeters) off the floor. Or space poly spots along the floor and ask the children to pretend to leap from rock to rock in a raging river. Don't place the poly spots too far apart; young children take "falling into the river" very seriously.

Gallop

The gallop is performed with an uneven rhythm. It is a combination of a walk and a run in which one foot leads and the other plays catch-up. Children will lead with the preferred foot long before they feel comfortable leading with the other foot.

Some young children learn this skill most easily when they can hear the gallop's rhythm. To provide this, play Gallop! with the children, in which you clap or beat out the appropriate rhythm on a hand drum. Among the musical possibilities is Ed Durlacher's recording, *Rhythms*, available from Educational Activities, Inc. (see appendix B).

Another possibility for teaching the gallop is a game called Fox and Hound in which the children pretend the lead foot is the fox and the back foot is the hound trying to catch the fox (Hammett, 1992). The fox always gets away. Eventually the feet reverse roles. Hammett recommends pipe cleaners shaped like fox ears attached to the shoes to help the children remember which is the lead foot. You can also invite the children to pretend to be horses or cowboys or cowgirls riding horses.

Hop

A hop propels the body upward from a takeoff on one foot (heel-ball-toe) to a landing on the same foot (toe-ball-heel). The free leg doesn't touch the ground.

Children are generally able to hop at about age four. To help them maintain the balance necessary for successful hopping, encourage them to lean slightly in the direction of the support (hopping) leg. This shifts the center of gravity. If a student continues to have problems with balance, hold his hand on the side of the raised leg or pair the child with someone who is hopping well. Your students should practice hopping on both the preferred and the nonpreferred foot.

Just as with jumping, ropes and hoops are useful props. The students can hop back and forth over a single rope and eventually two parallel ropes. They can also hop side to side, beginning at one end of the rope and continuing on toward the other. They then reverse direction and repeat the exercise on the other foot. With a hoop, the child hops in and out, all the way around. Having completed the circle, he reverses direction and repeats on the other foot.

Slide

This locomotor skill is a gallop performed sideward. One foot leads and the other plays catch-up, and the uneven rhythm remains the same as in the gallop. Because facing in one direction and moving in another is difficult for young children, they'll learn to slide much later than they learn to gallop. Once students learn to slide, they should practice it in both directions.

Often the easiest way for children to learn the slide is in a group circle, holding hands. In the activity Group Slide, children first circle in one direction and then the other as they would while playing Ring Around the Rosie. You can also demonstrate a slide for them, standing with your back to them and leading with the same foot they do, or facing them and leading with the opposite foot.

Skip

A combination of a step and a hop, the skip, like the gallop and the slide, has an uneven rhythm. With more emphasis placed on the hop than the step, the overall effect is a light, skimming motion during which the feet only momentarily leave the ground (step-*hop*, step-*hop*). The lead foot alternates. For many children, skipping initially on one side only is a normal developmental stage. Most children acquire the ability to skip on both sides at about five-and-a-half.

Possibilities for teaching the skip include providing rhythmic accompaniment, holding the child's hand and skipping with him, demonstration and imitation, and breaking down the components of the movement. To break down the movement, invite the children to walk and hop, walk and hop while chanting the appropriate rhythm. You'll likely find that different techniques work with different children.

Step-Hop

Like the skip, the step-hop combines a step and a hop, each with the same time value (step-hop, step-hop). It's performed with an even rhythm, and the lead foot alternates.

This step is used often in folk dances and is included here because, like a skip, it's a combination of basic locomotor movements. It's also a common movement (it can even be part of a layup shot in basketball), and it is developmentally appropriate for primary-grade students.

Introduce the step-hop to your students by providing an even 1-2 beat with your hands or on a drum and asking them to practice combining steps and hops, as many of each as they want. Gradually suggest that they reduce the number until they're performing just one of each, alternating between the two. Can they match their steps and hops to your beats and later to a piece of music in a 2/4 meter?

Nonlocomotor Skills

Nonlocomotor skills are movements performed in place, while standing, kneeling, sitting, or lying. Sometimes called *axial movement*, they involve the axis of the body rotating around a fixed point. Some textbook authors label them *nonmanipulative skills*, and others call them *nontraveling skills*.

Nonlocomotor movements shouldn't be considered only as exercises or warm-ups. Rather, they can serve as "points of departure for exploration and as instruments for creative expression" (Murray, 1975, p. 129). Many nonlocomotor skills, however, can certainly serve in both capacities.

It is difficult to list the nonlocomotor skills in a progressive order because many of them are acquired at approximately the same point in a child's development. Still, some are more challenging than others. The following list represents a general developmental progression of nonlocomotor skills, each with sample activities.

Stretch

A stretch extends the body, its parts, and one joint or several joints vertically, horizontally, or to any point between. This nonlocomotor skill, perhaps more than any other, is commonly regarded as an exercise. Frequently used as a warm-up, stretching actually better serves as a cool-down, preventing the contraction of exercised muscles.

Exploration of stretching aligns perfectly with the children's exploration of their personal space. As they stretch toward the ceiling, forward, backward, and to the side—while standing, kneeling, sitting, and lying—they discover the boundaries of their personal space while becoming familiar with this nonlocomotor skill. Arms, legs, torso, and even the neck can all stretch.

Bend

A bend uses ball-and-socket or hinge joints to bring two adjacent parts of the body together, generally toward the body's center. In addition to the body as a whole, many body parts can bend, including arms, fingers, legs, and neck. Bending and stretching are natural partners because, once a body part has been bent, it must straighten again.

Challenge your students to discover how many body parts can bend and in how many different ways by playing Stretch and Bend. Invite them to experiment with bending the waist, arms, and legs while kneeling, crouching, sitting, and lying on backs, tummies, and sides. To explore and contrast bending and stretching, use imagery the children can relate to. Possibilities include asking them to do the following:

- Stretch as though picking fruit from a tall tree.
- Flop like a rag doll.
- Stretch as though waking up and yawning.
- Bend over as though tying your shoes.
- Stretch to put something on a high shelf.
- Bend to pat a dog, then a cat.
- Stretch to shoot a basketball through a hoop.
- Bend to pick up a coin from the floor.
- Stretch as though climbing a ladder.

! TRY THIS

In the following challenges (Exploring Bending and Stretching) the skills are made more difficult because you are asking the children to bend or stretch more than one body part at a time. When they're ready to handle these challenges, invite your students to do the following:

- Stretch one arm high and the other low (one toward the ceiling and the other toward the floor).
- Bend one arm while stretching the other one high (low, out to the side).
- Reach both arms to the right, then to the left.
- Reach one arm to the side and the other toward the ceiling.
- On hands and knees, stretch one leg behind you and one arm forward.
- Lying on your back, stretch one leg and bend the other.
- Stretch one leg long and the other toward the ceiling.

- Bend to pick vegetables or flowers from the garden.
- Stretch as though reaching for a star.

Sit

A sit moves the body from any level to a position in which the body's weight rests on the buttocks or primarily on the outer thigh. Although young children certainly know how to sit, exploring the ways it's possible to get into a sitting position can enhance body and spatial awareness.

Ask the children to practice moving to a sitting position from standing, kneeling, and lying, with and without the help of the hands and at various tempos onto the buttocks or onto one thigh or the other. Here are two games that involve sitting. Cooperative Musical Chairs sets a goal of finding a way to share the remaining chairs rather than eliminating players. In Sitting in the Dark, chairs are arranged in a circle, facing outward, with at least 12 inches (30 centimeters) of space between them. The children, each standing in front of a chair, close their eyes. You then issue directions such as "Take two steps forward," or "Take one jump forward." The children do as directed and then reverse the process—without opening their eyes or turning around—and try to get back to their chair to sit down. This is a great exercise for spatial awareness and draws attention to the sense of sight, placing it in the content area of science.

Shake

A shake is a vibratory movement involving tension and relaxation. It can be performed by the whole body as well as by individual parts. Children love to shake because they view it as a somewhat silly movement. Shaking is also an excellent warm-up activity because it gently increases blood flow to the muscles.

Invite the children to shake the body as a whole. Then challenge them to find out how many body parts can shake. Does the number of parts that can shake change when the body goes from standing to kneeling to sitting to lying positions? To use imagery to explore shaking, ask the children to shake in the following ways:

- Like Jell-O when the bowl is moved
- Like a baby's rattle
- Like a leaf in the wind
- As though very cold
- As though very scared

Turn

A turn is a partial or complete rotation of the body around an axis causing a shift in weight placement. Turns can be executed in dozens of ways—on

Figure 4.4   These students are turning at different levels.

a variety of body parts, at a variety of levels, clockwise and counterclockwise (see figure 4.4).

Until your students are familiar with *left* and *right,* or *clockwise* and *counterclockwise,* it's best to simply ask them to turn first in one direction and then the other direction, using room markers to indicate the desired direction. For example, you might ask the children to turn toward the door, the storage closet, or the windows. When the children are developmentally ready, you can use the terms right and left and clockwise and counterclockwise to describe the direction in which they're turning.

The elements of space and time are useful in the exploration of this skill. Invite the children to turn slowly and quickly, in both directions, and at high and low levels. On what parts other than the feet can the children turn? Possibilities include the knees, bottom, tummy, and back. Can the children discover body parts that turn? Possibilities here are the head and upper torso (but neither can make a complete turn).

Rock and Sway

Although the rock and the sway share the common trait of transferring weight from one part of the body to another, they are essentially different. A rock is the more forceful of the two, using greater muscle tension and suspension. The feet typically leave the ground in a rock. A sway is an easy, relaxed motion that sustains rather than suspends. The feet typically stay on the ground in a sway.

It's fun for the children to practice swaying and rocking while holding hands in a circle or line. As an alternative, they can place their hands on one another's shoulders. Explore the continuum from light to strong (the element of force) by beginning with a gentle sway, gradually increasing the force of the sway until it becomes a rocking motion. Reverse the process until the children are once again swaying gently.

Appropriate imagery includes swaying like flowers, trees, or grass in the breeze. Rocking horses or rocking chairs convey the idea that rocking can be performed forward and backward in addition to side to side.

Swing

A swing creates an arc or a circle around a stationary base. It generally requires impulse and momentum, except perhaps when the swinging part is merely released to the force of gravity, as when an arm is dropped from overhead. Swinging movement can be executed by the body as a whole, by the upper or lower torso alone, and by the head, arms, and legs (one at a time, unless the body is suspended off the ground).

Demonstrate swinging movement with a jump rope held suspended in a vertical line. Then challenge the children to discover how many parts of the body can swing, encouraging them to explore swinging back and forth and side to side. Images that lend themselves to swinging include a clock pendulum, an elephant's trunk, a bell in a bell tower, windshield wipers, and a playground swing or flying trapeze. Any of these can be demonstrated with the body as a whole or with an individual body part such as an arm.

Twist

Unlike a turn, which rotates the whole body, a twist rotates part of the body around an axis. The neck, trunk, arms, and legs are the body parts most easily twisted. Wrists, ankles, shoulders, and hips can be twisted to a lesser extent.

Challenge the children to discover how many ways they can twist their bodies and body parts, perhaps to the accompaniment of pop tunes like "Peppermint Twist" or Dire Straits' "Twisting by the Pool." To incorporate imagery, invite the children to twist in these ways:

- Like the inside of a washing machine
- Like a screwdriver being used
- Like a wet dishrag being wrung
- As though wiping their bottoms with towels
- As though digging a little hole in the sand with a foot
- As though drying their bottom with a towel and digging a little hole in the sand with a foot at the same time (This may require a demonstration.) (Pica, 2000)

Dodge

A dodge generally uses the whole body as it shifts quickly and forcefully to avoid an object or person moving toward it. When combined with the run, the dodge becomes a locomotor skill. However, it is often performed from a stationary position, where it may involve other nonlocomotor movements such as bending, stretching, twisting, and falling.

Imagery is helpful in introducing the dodge to young children. You can ask them to pretend to dodge a flying disc, such as a Frisbee, a limb falling from a tree, a snowball, or a lot of people on a crowded street or in a crowded department store.

Fall

A fall moves the body from a higher position to a prone (facedown), supine (faceup), or on-the-side lying position. Falls are often sudden, forceful movements, but they may also be executed slowly and limply. Either way, the body should be relaxed in order to prevent injury.

Introduce your students to the fall by concentrating first on collapsing. Try an activity in which they stand in their own personal space and make their bodies stiff and tight. At a signal from you, the children immediately let go of the tightness and collapse to the floor. They then rise in slow motion and make their bodies stiff again. Repeat the process several times (Sullivan, 1982). This is an excellent cool-down or relaxation exercise.

To incorporate imagery, ask the children to fall like a rag doll, a puppet released from its strings, bowling pins, raindrops, snowflakes, Humpty Dumpty from a wall, and a collapsing building.

Summary of Skills

As you can see, practicing nonlocomotor, as well as locomotor, skills contributes a great deal to the children's body and spatial awareness, while also increasing their movement repertoire. Nonlocomotor skills—so often viewed as insignificant in comparison with gross motor skills—certainly warrant inclusion in your curriculum.

Using the Elements of Movement

As mentioned previously, motor skills can be considered among the *verbs* of movement education. And just as we modify verbs in language, we can modify these verbs with the *adverbs*—the elements of movement—space, shape, time, force, flow, and rhythm.

When the children practice locomotor and nonlocomotor skills, keep the elements of movement foremost in your mind. Yes, you can use imagery, music, and props to inspire variety in the children's practice. But it is through the movement elements that children have the greatest opportunity to fully experience each skill and its many possibilities. Not every movement element will be applicable to each skill. However, if you run through them

a   b

Figure 4.5   Contrasting forces of movement: *(a)* tiptoeing and *(b)* stomping.

in your mind one at a time, you can discard those that aren't appropriate and apply those that are.

For instance, the many ways of walking were used earlier as an example. Figure 4.5 depicts an example of the element of force as it is applied to walking. With that locomotor skill, all six elements of movement can be applied. With skipping, on the other hand, if you consider the directions that are part of the element of space, you'll realize that *backward* and *sideward* aren't appropriate. Only *forward* makes sense here. Given that, you can challenge the students to practice skipping in a forward direction, exploring the three possible pathways: straight, curving, and zigzag. Because the action and position of the arms are specific and critical where the skip is concerned, you would probably eliminate the element of shape from the children's exploration. Likewise, because a skip is intended to be performed lightly and to a specific rhythm, you'd pass over the elements of force and rhythm as well. But you can and should challenge the children to skip both quickly and slowly, using the element of time, and you can even incorporate flow into their practice.

For a nonlocomotor skill like turning, directions and levels are appropriate. Shape also applies: Challenge the students to create various body shapes as they turn. Time and force, to a certain extent, apply. And flow is appropriate because turns can be uninterrupted or stopped and begun again. To reinforce rhythm, ask your elementary students to complete a 360-degree turn in eight counts, for example.

Here's another example. If you are working on jumping, ask the children to practice jumping in the following ways:

- In place, forward, backward, to one side, to the other side (directions in *space*)
- Just barely coming off the floor, as high as possible (levels in *space*)
- In straight, curving, or zigzagging lines (pathways in *space*)
- Slowly, quickly (*time*)
- Lightly, heavily (*force*)
- With pauses—for example, jump-jump-stop, jump-jump-stop (*flow*)
- Matching the beat of your hand claps (*rhythm*)

The practice of extending movement experiences with the elements of movement will require your concentration at first, just as the movements themselves will for the children. But just as movement skills eventually become automatic for your students, so, too, will the use of movement elements for you.

REMEMBER THIS

Once students have acquired and begun to refine these fundamental movement skills, experiencing them in a variety of ways through the use of the elements of movement, they will be ready to begin tackling more complex movements, including combinations of skills and manipulative skills and the game, sport, gymnastic, and dance skills they will encounter in later grades.

- Asking children to perform skills they have little hope of mastering often leads to frustration and failure, which can lead to a distaste for physical activity.
- Maturation takes care of only part of the process of motor skill development. Thus, many children never achieve mature patterns for many motor skills.
- Each new skill progresses through stages of development.
- Motor development is age related but not age dependent.
- Keep the elements of movement in mind as children practice motor skills.

5

Fitness for Young Children

Promoting lifelong fitness is a priority among physical education professionals, especially now that we're in the midst of a childhood obesity crisis and a period in which children lead more sedentary lives than in any other time in history. Currently, one third of American children and youth are either obese or at risk of becoming obese. Over the past 30 years, the obesity rate has nearly tripled for children ages 2 to 5 years (from 5 to 14 percent) and youth ages 12 to 19 years (from 5 to 17 percent), and quadrupled for children ages 6 to 11 years (from 4 to 19 percent) (Institute of Medicine, 2006). Nine million American children are overweight (Ogden et al., 2002), and there is no evidence that the number of overweight children is decreasing (Hedley et al., 2004). Keith Geiger, former president of the National Education Association, has commented that we are raising the first generation of children who are less healthy than their parents.

You may feel, therefore, that you should emphasize fitness over fundamentals in your program. The truth, however, is that the two are not mutually exclusive; you can promote fitness *while* facilitating motor skill development. Moreover, children who achieve competence and confidence in their motor abilities are more likely to become adults who keep moving. And that means they're more likely to be fit for life.

In this chapter we explore the five health-related fitness factors, which are also the factors most developmentally appropriate for young children, and explore the ways in which you can promote them. But, first, let's look at what fitness for young children involves.

Definitions of Fitness

Everyone wants to be physically fit. But what exactly does that mean? How do the experts define it? The President's Council on Physical Fitness and Sports (2000) says physical fitness is

the ability to perform daily tasks vigorously and alertly, with energy left over for enjoying leisure-time activities and meeting emergency demands. It is the ability to endure, to bear up, to withstand stress, to carry on in circumstances where an unfit person could not continue, and is a major basis for good health and well-being.

The National Association for Sport and Physical Education (NASPE) describes physical fitness as "a condition where the body is in a state of well-being and readily able to meet the physical challenges of everyday life" (NASPE, 2002, p. 18).

As you might imagine, physical fitness is a personal matter; it differs from one person to another. That's because it's subject to several factors. Some, like gender, age, and heredity, can't be changed. According to a study of 4,000 families conducted by York University in Ontario, Canada, people inherit at least 50 percent of their flexibility, strength, endurance, and speed from their parents because characteristics such as blood volume, muscle development, and heart size are determined genetically (Katzmarzyk et al., 2000).

Other factors, including personal habits, diet, and physical activity levels, can and do affect fitness but require effort. If your students are to have healthy, active, productive lives, they will have to learn to make the most of those elements that can't be changed and to make an effort in those that can be. This is particularly relevant where children are concerned. The more active children are—and stay—the more likely they are to be fit, because active children tend to become active adults. In contrast, one study determined that only two percent of inactive children went on to become active as adults (Activity and Health Research, 1992).

One thing we know for sure about physical fitness is that it's fleeting. It can't be maintained without continued attention. And if that is going to happen, you need to understand that, especially where children are concerned, fitness is an ongoing *process*, not a product to be obtained once and for all. Perhaps most important, if this process is to succeed, you can't apply adult concepts of physical fitness and exercise to children.

Fitness in Early Childhood

If you envision a weekly regimen of cardiovascular and strength-training exercises to conduct with your students, you will have to rethink your plan, because that will seem more like yucky-tasting medicine than fun to kids. And unless it's fun, they won't be interested. Also, children won't exercise for the same reasons adults do.

Most adults exercise for the sake of their health or because they want to look good. Children should *never* be encouraged to exercise because it will make them look good, even if weight or obesity is an issue. Emphasizing exercise for the sake of appearance places the wrong value on physical activity and on appearance. Body image is especially important to keep in mind where young girls are concerned. Stephanie Dolgoff (n.d.) reported in an article on the Sesame Street Web site that in a 1991 study of more than 1,000 first- through third-grade girls in Indiana, 42 percent of them already preferred body shapes different from and thinner than their own. And of 3,175 fifth- through eighth-graders in a 1993 South Carolina study, more than 50 percent of the girls wanted to lose weight, regardless of whether or not they were heavy.

As far as health benefits are concerned, unlike adults, young children live very much in the moment. They're simply incapable of projecting themselves into the future. So you can't expect your students to exercise because it will ensure they'll be healthier at age 40 or they'll look and feel better at 60. Even if you explain that exercise will make them healthier *right now*, you're not likely to get an enthusiastic response. These are all adult concepts and adult goals that are beyond a young child's cognitive and emotional capabilities.

 CONSIDER THIS

It's your job to educate your students, but lecturing isn't likely to have much of an impact on young children. You'll make the greatest impression mostly by example and by offering a well-placed sentence or two. For example, as you stretch out, state "It's important to stretch after exercising so your muscles don't get all bunched up." Or, to stimulate the children's natural curiosity by saying "Wow, dancing like that really got my heart pumping. It's good for your health to do that sometimes. Is your heart going faster, too?"

Even if you could convince your students of the need for daily or three-times-a-week exercise and you were right there alongside them working up a sweat while all of you were getting into shape, any results would still most likely be temporary. The reason? If physical activity is something imposed on children, they'll probably stop doing it as soon as the choice is theirs to make. Then any benefits gained will soon be lost. Fitness is fleeting.

Also, if you reward your students for time spent in physical activity with stickers, ribbons, or stars, what happens when rewards are no longer forthcoming? What happens when a child has grown up and is on his own and there is no immediate payoff for dragging himself out of bed half an hour early to work out or for hitting the road for a jog after a long day in class or at work?

Two studies serve as excellent cautionary tales. In the first, adult women who'd recently joined a health club met with instructors to discuss their activity preferences. They were then randomly placed into one of two groups: one with perceived choice and one with perceived lack of choice. Although the activities assigned to them were actually those they said they preferred, the women in the so-called no-choice group thought their instructor had determined their activities. Six weeks later the women in the perceived-choice group had higher attendance and expressed greater intent to continue their enrollment (Thompson and Wankel, 1980).

The second study looked at the effect of rewarding children to play on a piece of popular equipment: the balance board. The researchers' hypothesis was that the children would perceive receiving a trophy, an extrinsic reward, for performing on the balance board as controlling. And, sure enough, the children who were rewarded with trophies were later less inclined to play on the board during free-choice times than those who'd expected no rewards (Orlick and Mosher, 1978).

What can educators learn from these studies? When people, whether children or adults, do something that's not their choice, they're less willing to do it. And when they do something for a reward, they're likely to stop doing it once the reward is no longer available. Reward and recognition also promote a product-oriented view of fitness. Once received, the process is finished. And as we know, *finished* is not possible.

The goal, of course, is to ensure lifelong fitness. That means your students will have to grow up with a love of physical activity and the way it makes them feel. You can get them off to the best possible start by ensuring that fitness is *fun,* which is linked to *intrinsic* motivation.

What besides fun constitutes intrinsic motivation for children? There are three major factors: choice, curiosity, and developmentally appropriate activities. As seen in the studies cited, choice is a major ingredient. Even the youngest children benefit from being part of the decision-making process. Children involved in the process from the start are more likely to continue, even after an adult is no longer participating (Cooper, 1999). So any time you can offer your students choice, for example, with the activities they'll perform at different stations, the more they'll enjoy themselves.

? CONSIDER THIS

- Approximately 10 percent of children ages two to five are overweight (Ogden et al., 2002).

- About 60 percent of obese 5- to 10-year-olds show at least one heart disease risk factor, including hypertension and elevated cholesterol, and 25 percent show two or more risk factors (Freedman et al., 2001). (A variety of definitions can be used to determine childhood obesity. The standard definition of obesity is when a person is more than 20 percent over ideal weight.)

- Studies by the Institute for Aerobic Research (1987) indicate that the first signs of arteriosclerosis appear at age five.

- Sedentary lifestyles among adults are a major health problem in the United States, with an estimated 300,000 deaths a year caused by low levels of activity and fitness (Cooper, 1999), placing sedentary living in the same risk category as smoking cigarettes or driving drunk.

Using movement exploration, or divergent problem solving, is a wonderful way to offer children choice because there are several possible responses to each challenge, and the children respond according to their level of ability and skill development. When you acknowledge the multiple responses you get, the children realize that it's okay to find their own way.

A second factor contributing to intrinsic motivation for children is curiosity. When an activity provokes curiosity, children will participate in order to satisfy their curiosity (Hinson, 1995). Would your students be curious about what happens to their heart rate after a run around the gym or about how many sounds they can hear in a walk around the track?

Finally, developmentally appropriate activities that are neither too easy nor too difficult also help foster intrinsic motivation. Children become bored with activities that are too easy and frustrated by those that are too challenging. So it's important to know what your students are developmentally ready to do.

Fitness Factors

Physical fitness consists of two components: **health-related fitness** and **skill-related fitness.** Skill-related fitness incorporates balance, agility, coordination, power, speed, and reaction time. Although some of these abilities will result from your work with the students, it is the health-related factors that are developmentally appropriate for young children and thus require your focus. These factors are cardiorespiratory endurance, muscular strength, muscular endurance, flexibility, and body composition.

Each health-related fitness factor is defined, and suggestions for incorporating them into your curriculum are provided. Table 5.1 summarizes the five factors and lists sample activities.

Table 5.1   Health-Related Fitness Factors

Factor	Definition	Sample activity
Cardiorespiratory endurance	Ability of heart and lungs to supply oxygen	Dancing to moderate- to fast-paced music
Muscular strength	Ability to exert force with a single maximum effort	Jumping
Muscular endurance	Muscles' ability to continue contracting over time	Jumping continuously
Flexibility	Range of motion around joints	Bending and stretching
Body composition	Percentage of lean body tissue	Aerobic and muscle-strengthening movements

Cardiorespiratory Endurance

Cardiorespiratory endurance is the ability of the heart and lungs to supply oxygen and nutrients to the muscles. Someone with great cardiorespiratory endurance has a strong heart that is larger and pumps more blood per beat than the heart of someone who is not fit. Cardiorespiratory endurance improves when a person exercises regularly. Typically, it's aerobic exercise that improves cardiorespiratory fitness, but where young children are concerned, you can't think of *aerobics* in the same way that you do for adults.

Young children, particularly before the age of six, aren't made for long, uninterrupted periods of strenuous activity. So expecting them to jog, walk briskly, or perform a structured exercise regimen for 20 to 30 minutes is not only unrealistic but could be damaging. Their skeletal structures and organs are still too immature for such exertion, and young children cannot rid their bodies of heat as efficiently as can older children and adults. At the very least, it can instill an intense dislike of physical activity. Rather, when considering appropriate aerobic activities for children, think along the lines of moderate to vigorous play and movement. Physical activity that's moderately intense will increase the heart rate and breathing somewhat, while vigorous movement takes a lot more effort and will result in a noticeable increase in breathing. (The resting heart rate of a six-year-old is typically 95 beats a minute, as compared with the 72 beats for an adult. As with adults, children should still be able to talk while performing aerobic activities.)

Walking, marching, playing tag, dancing to moderate- to fast-paced music, and jumping rope all fall under the heading of moderately to vigorously intense exercise for children. It's anything that keeps the children moving continuously, sometimes strenuously and sometimes less so. Playing Follow the Leader to "Beep Beep" (mentioned in chapter 3 on page

 CONSIDER THIS

NASPE's *Physical Activity for Children: A Statement of Guidelines for Children Ages 5-12* (2004) emphasizes the appropriateness of intermittent, as opposed to prolonged, activity. The guidelines recommend bouts of developmentally appropriate physical activity adding up to 60 minutes on all or most days of the week. The guidelines additionally suggest the following:

- Some of the child's activity each day should be at moderate to vigorous levels, in periods lasting 10 to 15 minutes or more.
- Children should experience a *variety* of physical activities.
- Extended periods of inactivity should be discouraged.

38) is a great example of a developmentally appropriate aerobic activity for young children, as is pretending to be in a track meet. Even working with a parachute can be a good cardiovascular activity if it's vigorous enough and performed continuously.

Muscular Strength

Muscular strength is fairly self-explanatory and is described as the ability to exert force with a single maximum effort. Strong muscles are necessary not only for performing certain tasks, like throwing for distance, hanging and swinging, climbing, and carrying heavy books and groceries, but also for preventing injury and for maintaining proper posture. An added bonus is that increasing muscle strength also increases strength in tendons, ligaments, and bones.

Strength training, also known as resistance or weight training, is the best way to build muscular strength. But here again, you must view things differently than when discussing adults or even adolescents. Although there is much debate over the appropriateness of strength training for young children, experts agree on several points.

First, it's never a good idea to modify an adult strength-training program for children. Here are some of the reasons:

• Adults' bodies are fully developed; children's are not.

• Adults have long attention spans and the motivation to endure the monotony of repetitive exercises; children do not.

• Adults can follow specific instructions for proper form and understand the risks in handling strength-training equipment; children cannot.

As such, the best strength training for children involves the use of their own weight in physical activities they already perform (see figure 5.1), like jumping (a locomotor skill), playing Tug-of-War (an introductory manipulative skill), and hanging and swinging (gymnastic skills).

Perhaps you've seen photographs or news articles about children's fitness programs, showing very young children lifting weights that have been specially designed for kids. But here, too, most experts agree: Children under the age of eight shouldn't use weights or machines, child sized or not. The general rule of thumb is that only children mature enough to follow specific instructions and understand the risks and benefits of such training should handle strength-training equipment. Children should wait until they're 10, and preferably 12, to use equipment because before puberty they may not have the judgment necessary to use it safely (Cooper, 1999).

There's a good deal of interest in children's fitness right now and plenty of programs cropping up to take advantage of that interest. These programs heartily endorse the benefits of strength training, convincing parents that it will prevent injury and improve sport skills. And, yes, if children participate in organized sports without the requisite strength, strength-*related* activities *may* help prevent sport-related injuries. But strength training, handled improperly, can do more harm than good, particularly in children under six, who are most prone to injury. Muscle strains, especially in the low back, are the most common injury. And the truth is, the best way for children to improve their sport skills is to learn and practice their specific sport skills. Strength isn't a factor in movement and sport for young children; rather, skill level makes the greatest difference (Sayre and Gallagher, 2001).

Figure 5.1 Climbing uses a child's own weight to promote muscular strength.

If you're considering the pros and cons of strength training, here are some things you should know:

- Children should always begin by using the resistance of their own body weight. In addition to the examples cited earlier, this could include formal exercises such as heel raises (relevés, in dance terms), knee bends (pliés), curl-ups, leg lifts, and wall push-ups. If you ask your students to do such monotonous movements, find a way to make them fun. (See "Try This" on page 72.)

- If your six- to eight-year-old students participate in some sort of formal regimen, that regimen should include a warm-up, for example, jogging lightly in place to circulate blood throughout the body, and a cool-down such as holding gentle stretches for 10 to 12 seconds.

- The most appropriate apparatus for children is one *created* for children, not equipment originally designed for adults and then shrunk. (See appendix B for recommended equipment vendors.)

- Children benefit more from additional repetitions of moderate weight than from fewer repetitions of heavier weights.

- A knowledgeable adult should constantly monitor children participating in strength-training programs.

- Strength training may further elevate the blood pressure in children with hypertension.

Gains in strength, muscle size, and power are lost only six weeks after strength training is stopped (American Academy of Pediatrics, 2001). So, if children are to improve muscular strength, strength training must be continuous. And, honestly, the only way that's going to happen for young children is if it's part of what they naturally do and it's fun.

! TRY THIS

Jumping continuously can be tiring. And if it's being done just for the sake of jumping, it's not much fun. To give children a reason to jump, play Rabbits and 'Roos, in which they pretend to jump first like kangaroos and then like rabbits, alternating frequently. Before beginning, talk to the children about rabbits and kangaroos. Which is biggest? Which weighs the most? Young children enjoy pretending to be animals, and alternating between jumping heavily and jumping lightly makes it possible to sustain the movement longer.

When alternating between heel raises and knee bends, your students can pretend to be popcorn popping. And lifting and bicycling the legs can be much more enjoyable with jingle bands, Velcro bands with bells attached, strapped to the ankles. (When doing leg lifts, the children should raise one leg at a time to prevent strain to the low back.) Also, bicycling with a partner—both children lying on their backs with knees bent and soles of the feet together—makes this activity more fun.

Muscular Endurance

Muscular endurance is the muscles' ability to continue contracting for an extended time. In other words, it's about stamina. With enough stamina, a person can repeat movements, hold positions, or carry objects without tiring.

Obviously, muscular endurance is tied to muscular strength, so many of the same kinds of activities and exercises benefit both. However, muscular endurance also depends on skill level. A skilled person has the ability to perform movements in the most efficient manner; it comes naturally to her after years of practice. That means she can sustain movement for lengthier periods. A young child, by virtue of having fewer years of practice in most skills, will use the maximum force and contract more muscles than actually needed for the movement. Therefore, you can't expect her to last as long as a skilled mover.

Flexibility

Flexibility is the range of motion around joints. When people are flexible, they can stretch to put something on a high shelf, bend to tie a shoe, or sit cross-legged without effort or aches and pains. They can swing a tennis racket or a golf club, perform a layup in basketball, or reach for a high fly without fear of muscle strain, sprain, or spasm.

In general, girls tend to be more flexible than boys, who start to lose their flexibility at about age 10. Girls begin to lose flexibility at 12. But this doesn't have to happen. If children are physically active, they'll be flexible. But they also should be encouraged to work on their flexibility through gentle, static stretches that take a muscle just beyond its usual length (without pain!) and are held for at least eight seconds.

Of course, stretching just for the sake of stretching is boring—and point-less—to young children. They will, however, enjoy "painting" the inside of their "bubbles," which requires reaching high, low, and wide, and the bending and stretching exercise described in chapter 2, in which they pretend to do such things as bending to tie a shoe and reaching for a star (see figure 5.2). To encourage children to hold the stretches, chal-lenge them to pretend to do these activities in slow motion. Other ways to

Figure 5.2   Stretching is the best exercise for promoting flexibility.

promote flexibility include giving the children ribbon sticks and inviting them to move the ribbons high, low, and all around them (be sure they try it with both hands) and giving them stretch bands or stretchy sacks, such as Body Sox, into which children can fit their whole bodies, with which to experiment. You can also challenge students to play Bridges and Tunnels, in which they demonstrate bridges and tunnels with their bodies. How do they differ from each other? Which is usually the rounder of the two? Once they've had a chance to experiment with the possibilities, divide the class into two groups; half the children are tunnels, and the other half are cars or trains traveling through the tunnels. Allow enough time for the students to reverse roles.

Avoid two no-nos regarding stretching. First, children should work their own limbs through their range of motion; it's extremely easy for an adult or even another child to stretch a child's muscles and joints too far. Second, warn children against ballistic stretching (bouncing). It can cause small tears in the muscle fibers and is not as effective as static stretching.

Body Composition

The final component of health-related fitness is **body composition:** the body's makeup in terms of the percentage of fat, muscle, tissue, and bone, or the ratio of lean tissue to fat.

With childhood obesity becoming more of a problem as the years go by, a lot of attention is focused on body composition right now, so it's important to remember that weight alone isn't a good indicator of body composition. Some children are simply large boned. Also, muscle weighs more than fat. So it's possible for two children to have the same weight but very different body makeup, one possessing very little fat and the other too much. Generally, you can tell if a child has too much body fat by his or her appearance. But if you want to know for sure, determine the child's body mass index (BMI), which is a reliable indicator of body fatness for most children. The Web site for the Centers for Disease Control and Prevention (www.cdc.gov/nccdphp/dnpa/bmi) offers information on how to use BMI with children.

Physical activity, of course, is the key to reducing body fat; aerobic and muscle-strengthening movements offer the most benefit. A major study conducted in the United States showed that inactive preschool children were almost four times more likely than active preschoolers to enter first grade with increased body fatness (Moore et al., 1995).

⬤ REMEMBER THIS

As you can see, it is possible to promote physical fitness while developing motor skills. By combining the two, you ensure that your students will have the necessary skills and confidence to become lifelong movers. And by ensuring that your students find fitness fun, you can help combat obesity before it starts rather than once it's upon them.

- Active children are more likely than inactive children to become active adults.
- Physical fitness is an ongoing process.
- Adult concepts of physical fitness and exercise can't be applied to children.
- If physical activity is something children have had imposed on them or if they're rewarded for taking part in it, they're likely to stop the activity as soon as the choice is theirs to make or the reward no longer exists.
- Young children will be physically active only if it's fun and they're intrinsically motivated to participate in it.
- The health-related fitness factors—cardiorespiratory endurance, muscular strength, muscular endurance, flexibility, and body composition—should be the focus in early childhood.

Manipulative
Skills

In some physical education texts, manipulative skills are described as gross motor movements involving force imparted to or received from objects. Others characterize manipulative skills as activities using an implement, usually with the hands but sometimes with the feet or other body parts. In this book, **manipulative skills** are defined as any gross motor skill that usually involves an object.

In many PE programs, manipulative skills receive the most attention because they're sport-related and lend themselves to game playing. However, just by virtue of involving an object, manipulative skills are more challenging than basic locomotor and nonlocomotor skills and therefore should be introduced *after* children are comfortable with the basics. So, although this chapter is dedicated to manipulative skills, these skills are not emphasized the way they are in traditional PE books.

Again, early childhood physical education is unique. The overriding principle must be *fundamentals first*. This doesn't necessarily mean that you won't use objects in the early stages of the curriculum. On the contrary, equipment and props offer the children additional movement possibilities. Manipulating objects provides opportunities to move in new ways that require different levels of coordination and lets students become comfortable with objects. And focusing on the movement of a prop can alleviate self-consciousness and encourage children who might not otherwise want to participate.

However, the ability to manipulate an object should be secondary to the ability of the body to manipulate itself through space. And, as you can see, the use of props described in the previous paragraph has more to do with body and spatial awareness than with sports, which shouldn't be the focus of an early childhood physical education curriculum. So when your students are ready to begin acquiring and refining traditional manipulative skills, offer activities that provide ample experience with the skills without involving the cognitive or social and emotional issues central to sports, for which your young students are still not developmentally ready.

Nontraditional Manipulative Skills

Before you ask your students to practice traditional, sport-related manipulative skills, introduce them to activities that explore the skills with which they're already familiar, skills they've been performing since they were infants: pulling, pushing, lifting, and striking (with the arms alone). Initially, exploring these skills with imaginary objects allows children to become familiar with the body movement itself. It also offers ample opportunity for success. Following are definitions of the skills, along with sample activities.

Pull

A pull entails resistance and is used to move something from one place to another, toward the base of support. To complete this movement, the arms first extend and then usually bend. Pulling may be prolonged when it accompanies a locomotor movement, as when a child pulls a wagon behind him while walking.

Ask the children to pull something imaginary in the following ways:

- With both hands
- With one hand
- With alternating hands
- Toward them
- Strongly and hard (as though against great resistance)
- Lightly (against less resistance)
- Slowly, then quickly
- With short movements, then long

Push

A push moves something, also against resistance, from one place to another, *away* from the base of support. A push starts with the arms drawn in and continues until the arms are extended. The movement may be prolonged by combining it with a locomotor movement, as when a child pushes a box across the floor while walking. Pushing seems to be more difficult for young children than pulling (Sinclair, 1973).

Repeat the pulling challenges, but substitute pushing. Also ask the children to push forward, downward, upward, and sideward. To contrast pushing and pulling, ask the children to move as though they were doing the following:

- Pushing a swing
- Pulling a rope
- Pushing heavy furniture
- Pulling a kite
- Pushing a balloon into the air
- Pulling a wagon or sled
- Pushing a car stuck in mud or snow
- Pulling a balloon from the sky
- Pushing a shovel

Lift

A lift transports an object from one place to another by raising it. When the skill requires carrying an object, it becomes a locomotor movement as well. When moving from a low to a high level, children must bend the knees and then straighten them as they lift.

Ask the children to pretend to lift something very light, first with both hands, then with one, and finally with the other. Can they show you how it would look to move this object from low to high and from high to low? Now challenge them to repeat the process, pretending the object is very heavy. How does that make lifting different? What would it look like to lift something hot? What about something filled to the brim with liquid that must not spill? How about something round? Something sharp?

Strike

A strike is a strong movement of the arm (or arms) in any direction for the purpose of hitting an object. The arm must bend to initiate the strike, extending with both force and speed. When performed without an implement, such as a bat or hockey stick, the movement abruptly stops, with no follow-through in the arm motion.

Ask the children to pretend to strike a big bass drum, swing a bat, hammer a nail, chop wood, swat at a mosquito, and bounce a ball. Challenge them to try the following while standing, kneeling, and sitting:

- Strike the air with both arms.
- Strike with one arm; try it with the other arm.
- Strike with alternating arms.
- Strike upward (downward, sideward, forward).
- Strike with a long, short, and medium extension of the arms.

Introducing Equipment

Although college preparation courses in physical education emphasize gross motor coordination, teachers should provide both gross and fine motor activities within the movement curriculum. Inappropriate practice emphasizes "either gross or fine motor learning experiences to the exclusion of the other" (NASPE, 2000, p. 13).

Typically, when considering fine motor skills, people think of activities such as writing with an implement and using scissors, neither of which is normally associated with PE. But fine motor coordination, which develops later than gross motor coordination, involves the use of the small muscles that control the hands, fingers, and thumb in coordination with the eyes.

CONSIDER THIS

Appropriate Practices in Movement Programs for Young Children Ages 3-5 is a position statement of the National Association for Sport and Physical Education, developed by the Council on Physical Education for Children (COPEC). The document is intended to assist people who educate these children to

1. make developmentally appropriate decisions about curriculum and content;
2. make informed decisions about how content is presented;
3. evaluate existing curriculum and teaching methods;
4. advocate the improvement of existing programs; and
5. more fully integrate movement activities into existing curricula.

This document can be ordered by requesting stock no. 304-10232. It is also available online as a PDF document at www.aahperd.org/NASPE/peappropriatepractice/AppropriatePractices3-5.pdf.

Possessing fine motor coordination, therefore, is applicable to physical education. If for no other reason, it contributes to the children's ability to manipulate objects.

Fingerplays, rhymes in which children use their hands to act out the words, are one way to promote fine motor coordination. And you can perform fingerplays as part of warm-ups and cool-downs. "Where Is Thumbkin?" is a musical fingerplay that's a favorite among young children. Sit in a circle with the students and sing the song, inviting them to show you the whereabouts of Thumbkin, Pointer, Middle Finger, Ring Finger, Baby Finger, and the whole family.

If you want to promote fine motor coordination while specifically preparing children to manipulate objects, there are several activities and games that will do so. For example, opening and closing fingers one at a time helps improve hand strength and fine motor coordination. This activity, called Opening and Closing Fingers, may require a lot of repetition from your youngest students, but they'll still enjoy it. Have them curl their hands into loose fists. Then, as you count (very slowly at first) from 1 to 10, they uncurl their fingers one at a time. Reverse, counting 10 to 1, while the children curl one finger at a time back into their palms.

Ask the children to do finger push-ups by touching the tips of the fingers and thumb on one hand to the tips of the fingers and thumb on the other hand. They alternately stretch and bend (lengthen and shorten) the fingers without breaking contact between them. Accompany this exercise with a drum beat or hand clap or by calling out "stretch and bend." When the children are strong enough, ask them to stand facing a wall, about a foot away (30 centimeters) from it. With their arms bent and elbows at their sides, they lean forward and touch the wall with the tips of their fingers. They then do "push-ups" by alternately extending and bending their fingers.

Parachute games are an excellent way to help children become comfortable manipulating objects. Begin by inviting the children to rotate the parachute while they stand in place. By passing it to their right or left, your students will gain practice with gripping and handing off. Make sure they try it in both directions.

Making ripples that become increasingly bigger until they're large waves not only provides practice with gripping, but it also exercises the upper torso, something today's children have too little experience with. Place cotton balls, Styrofoam peanuts, or lightweight foam balls on the parachute and challenge your students to move the chute up and down in little waves while keeping all of the balls or peanuts on it. How high can they make the parachute go and still keep the objects from falling off? You can also play the game the opposite way: determining how quickly they can shake the objects off the parachute.

Two more challenging parachute games are Roll Around and Hole in One (Pica, 2006). To play Roll Around, place a single ball on the parachute and ask everyone to work together to try to roll the ball around the outer edge first in one direction and then in the other. To play Hole in One, place a ball that's smaller than the hole in the center of the chute on the parachute. The children work together to try to get the ball through the hole in the middle. Both of these games contribute significantly to fine motor and eye–hand coordination. They also involve cooperation, which places them in the content area of social studies.

Using ribbon sticks is another excellent way to promote fine motor coordination and to help children feel comfortable manipulating an object. Your students can use the sticks to "write" letters and numbers in the air and to "paint" lines, circles, and figure-eights. These are all wonderful activities that require crossing the body's midline. You can also play music in various styles and invite the children to discover how it makes the ribbon stick want to move. Phrasing your challenge in this way encourages even the shyest children to participate because the focus is on the prop and not on them.

❓ CONSIDER THIS

If, after handing out props, you allow the children a couple of minutes to play with them in any way they want, they will be more willing to listen to your instructions for using them.

To help the children become comfortable with balls specifically, play games that are clearly unrelated to sports. This should alleviate the pressure children often associate with winning and losing. In Over and Under, the children stand in a circle or line, each facing the back of another child. The first child hands the ball backward over her head to the next child, and so on down the line or around the circle (see figure 6.1). The children then stand with legs apart and pass the ball behind them, putting it between their legs and handing it to the next person. The final challenge is to pass the ball in alternating ways: one child passing it overhead and the next passing it through the legs (Pica, 2006).

Figure 6.1   Students play Over and Under, a game designed to help them get comfortable with ball handling.

In another activity the children stand in a circle and hand a small, easy-to-grip ball from one to another, all the way around the circle. To promote social studies and name recognition, children say their name as they receive the ball. Or, once the children know each other's names, they can call out the name of the person to whom they gently toss the ball. To promote counting skills (the content area of math), ask the first child with the ball to count "one" out loud as she passes the ball. The next child counts "two," and so on around the circle.

Remember that any activities you conduct that strengthen the children's hands or promote fine motor coordination will not only benefit the children in the gym but also in the classroom. And that helps you to advocate for your content area.

Traditional Manipulative Skills

Following are descriptions of the traditional manipulative skills, along with suggestions for exploring them with your young students. In early childhood, it's important that these skills not be associated with sports when they're first introduced.

Throw

Throwing consists of moving an object away from the body through the air by using the hands. Following the infant–toddler phase of throwing objects—tossing food and bottles overhand in a downward direction—children generally progress from a two-handed underhand throw to a one-handed underhand throw to a one-handed overhand throw (Kirchner, 2001). Often, the size and weight of the ball dictate the type of throws.

Accuracy is not the first objective when teaching young children to throw. Rather, they must initially become familiar with the throwing

! TRY THIS

To give children practice with underhand throwing, line up empty plastic soda bottles or plastic cones side by side and spaced far enough apart that plastic hoops tossed over them won't interfere with each other. Line up each child opposite a bottle or cone, only a short distance away, and give each child a hoop. Invite the children to try to toss their hoop over their cone or bottle. After an unsuccessful try, the children retrieve the hoop and try again. With each successful try, they can take a step farther away from the cone or bottle if they desire. If they don't succeed from the greater distance, they can step forward. What's most important is practicing the throwing motion.

action itself. Begin by providing foam or yarn balls and asking the children to practice throwing them against a wall from which they gradually move farther away at their own discretion. When the children are ready to move to a greater challenge, ask them to throw at a large target, such as into a large box or rubber trash barrel and eventually a hoop hung on the wall. As they become more proficient, challenge the children to gradually move farther away from the targets. You can also decrease the size of the targets.

To provide practice with overhand throwing, modify the game of Messy Backyard. Make a line with tape, chalk, or rope. Divide the children into two groups, one on each side of the line. Place an equal number of chiffon scarves on each side of the line. Set a timer. At your signal, the children race to pick up the scarves on their side of the line and throw them onto the other side of the line. When time is up, count the number of scarves on each side, then divide them equally and start over.

Kick

Kicking imparts force to an object, usually a ball, with the leg and foot, most often the side or top of the instep. This skill requires eye–foot coordination, which usually is not fully developed until age 9 or 10, body control and coordination, and accuracy of force and direction. Children should practice kicking for distance frequently to develop a mature kicking pattern; kicking for accuracy should not be a concern until after children have mastered the mature pattern (Gallahue, 1993).

Because beach balls are difficult to miss, start with these. Ask the children to kick them any way they can, both with the preferred and the nonpreferred foot. With more skilled children, replace the beach ball with a large foam ball. Following attempts to kick in any way possible, challenge students to kick the ball at a wall from which they gradually move farther away and, later, under and then over a suspended jump rope.

Ball Roll

Like throwing, ball-rolling involves moving a ball away from the body with the hands, but rather than through the air, the ball travels along the ground. Ball-rolling skills are most often associated with games like bowling and kickball but are also used in activities such as bocce, shuffleboard, and curling. The basic pattern is also seen in underhand throwing, including pitching in softball, and lifesaving rope-tossing activities (Gallahue, 1993).

As with throwing, accuracy is not the initial objective in teaching children to roll a ball. Begin by asking them to roll balls of various sizes at the wall. When the children feel comfortable with this, substitute targets such as plastic bowling pins and empty soda bottles, beginning with large balls and gradually decreasing their size.

❗ TRY THIS

Typically, bowling requires tremendous eye–hand coordination and a lot of waiting. But young children aren't particularly adept at either. Instead, play this game with the students in pairs and with larger objects than the standard bowling ball and pins.

To play, arrange two or three soda bottles in close proximity to each other for each pair of children, and give each pair a beach ball or large playground ball. One child stands near the "pins" while the other rolls the ball and tries to knock the bottles down. The second child retrieves the ball while the first resets the pins. Then the second child takes a turn at bowling. The children continue in this manner, taking turns for as long as they stay interested (Pica, 2006).

Volley

Volleying is defined as striking an object in an upward direction with the hands or other body parts, excluding the feet. Body parts typically used for volleying include the head, arms, and knees, as witnessed during a game of soccer. Accurate visual tracking is necessary for this skill.

When working on volleying with young children, use lightweight, colorful objects like balloons and beach balls to help ensure success. Provide a medium or large balloon for each child and challenge the class to try hitting them upward and forward with the hands. The next step is to volley the balloon with just the preferred hand, later trying it with the nonpreferred hand. Next challenge the children to volley the balloon with different body parts. How many can they volley with?

Another activity is to give each *pair* of children a balloon and challenge them to keep it in the air. There's one stipulation: Neither child can touch the balloon twice in a row.

Bounce

Bouncing, sometimes referred to as dribbling, is accomplished by striking an object, most often a ball, in a downward direction with one or both hands. The developmental progression seems to be "(1) bouncing and catching, (2) bouncing and ineffective slapping at the ball, (3) basic dribbling with the ball in control of the child, (4) basic dribbling with the child in control of the ball, and (5) controlled dribbling with advanced abilities" (Gallahue, 1993, p. 315). Although bouncing a ball doesn't have much application later in life, it's an excellent tool for developing eye–hand coordination.

Beginning with large playground balls or small beach balls, challenge the children to bounce and catch with two hands, varying the number of bounces between catches. Once they've become proficient with this, challenge them to bounce continuously with two hands. The final challenge is to bounce with the preferred hand and eventually with the nonpreferred hand.

Catch

The catching skill of receiving and controlling an object with the hands requires children to focus on the approaching object and make the adjustments necessary to receive it. Catching is often more difficult for some children than others because they fear the object as it approaches. Using soft, colorful objects such as scarves, beanbags, balloons, or yarn balls and large, soft beach balls or foam balls can alleviate the fear *and* make visual tracking easier.

Children begin by catching their own bounced ball. Catching from someone who is able to throw accurately is the next challenge. Once children achieve a certain measure of success, they can try to catch an object they have tossed into the air themselves. Large chiffon scarves, sometimes called juggling or dancing scarves, are perfect for this because they're colorful, lightweight, and slow moving.

Strike

Striking refers to imparting force to an object by using an implement such as a racket, paddle, or bat. This is one of the last skills children develop because visual tracking isn't refined until the upper elementary years and because eye–hand coordination is more challenging at greater distances from the body; the difficulty of striking increases with the length of the implement (Graham, Holt/Hale, and Parker, 2003). However, by striking lightweight objects with short-handled implements, young children can experience success with this skill.

When initially exploring this skill, the object and child are stationary. For example, ask the child to strike a beach ball that is sitting on the floor with a large, lightweight bat or hit a ball off a cone or tee. Next, the child remains still and the object moves (e.g., the child hits a pitched beach ball with a paddle or large, lightweight bat). The final challenge occurs when the object and the child move; for example, the child keeps a ball in the air with a paddle.

Dribble

Although dribbling can refer to manipulating a ball with the hands, the term here refers to the manipulation of a ball with the *feet*. Force is imparted to the ball horizontally along the ground, but unlike kicking, in which the ball can also travel in a vertical direction, the goal is not to use force to gain distance. Rather, the child controls the ball by keeping it close to the feet. Dribbling, like kicking, requires eye–foot coordination and a great deal of body control.

Children should first practice dribbling with a beanbag, which is less dynamic than a ball. Once they're able to do so, provide a pathway, and later an obstacle course, for them to dribble through. Encourage them to alternate their feet. Later, using a small beach ball or playground ball (8 to 12 inches [20 to 30 centimeters] in diameter), the children begin controlling the ball with the inside and outside of their feet.

➡ REMEMBER THIS

Manipulative skills are more challenging than basic locomotor and nonlocomotor skills and should be explored after children are comfortable with the basics. In a developmentally appropriate early childhood PE curriculum, the manipulation of objects should be secondary to the ability of the body to manipulate itself through space. With that in mind, here are additional points to remember:

- Pretending to perform manipulative skills—beginning with the nontraditional skills of pulling, pushing, lifting, and striking with the hands—allows children to experience the *feel* of these movements and also to experience success with them.

- When first introducing objects to your students, it should be for the purpose of providing opportunities for them to move in new ways.

- Fine motor coordination should be a part of early childhood physical education. Using parachutes, ribbon sticks, and easy-to-grip balls contributes to fine motor coordination.

- There are many ways to introduce your students to traditional manipulative skills that are unrelated to sports. Using these nontraditional methods allows for maximum success and enjoyment.

7

Linking the Gym
With the Classroom

Over the past few decades, standardized testing has increasingly become the tool by which the success of schools and their students is measured. The No Child Left Behind Act of 2001 is the latest federal legislation to focus on standards-based educational reform, and its implementation has stepped up the clamor for more accountability and, as a result, more "seatwork." The current emphasis in education—even the child's earliest education—is on academics, with emergent literacy and mathematics in the forefront. Physical education specialists, consequently, face more pressure than ever to advocate for their subject. This may be especially true in the Western world, where many still fail to see the connection between mind and body. When considering PE, many tend to think only in terms of the child's physical development. *Cognitive* development doesn't come readily to mind. Because of this attitude and the belief that the functions of the mind are more important than those of the body, physical education and even recess are being eliminated in favor of more academic time.

Of course, PE professionals know that the body matters, too! They're also aware of studies revealing that children who engage in physical activity show improved academic performance, including higher test scores and a better attitude toward school (Hannaford, 2005; Jensen, 2000a). Recent brain research has determined that because a child's earliest learning is based on motor development, so is much of the learning that follows. The cerebellum, the part of the brain previously associated only with motor control, is actually involved in a great deal of cognitive activity (Jensen, 2000a). Jensen cites numerous studies that have demonstrated a connection between the cerebellum and the cognitive functions of memory, spatial orientation, attention, language, and decision making, among others.

Thanks also to advances in brain research, it's clear that most of the brain is activated during physical activity, much more so than when doing seatwork. In fact, according to Jensen, sitting for more than 10 minutes at a stretch "reduces our awareness of physical and emotional sensations and increases fatigue," which results in reduced concentration and, in children, discipline problems (2000b, p. 30).

Movement, on the other hand, increases the capacity of blood vessels and possibly even their number, allowing for the delivery of oxygen, water, and glucose, otherwise known as "brain food," to the brain. And this can't help but optimize the brain's performance.

Perhaps of greatest importance for the purposes of this chapter is the fact that, despite the ever-changing educational priorities of adults, children haven't changed. They are still experiential learners who retain more when they use multiple senses in the learning process (Fauth, 1990), they still need to physically experience concepts to fully understand them, and movement is still the young child's preferred mode of learning. Simply put, children learn best through active involvement. And there's no better place for active involvement than in your gym.

Typically, the early childhood and early elementary curricula include experiences in four major content areas: language arts (emergent literacy), mathematics, science, and social studies. If the children are fortunate, in addition to physical education they are also offered experiences in art and music. This chapter looks at these six content areas and the themes and concepts they traditionally encompass. Following a brief discussion of each subject are suggestions for exploring many of its concepts through movement. You may be surprised at how much movement has in common with these classroom topics and how easy it is to integrate them into your program without compromising your objectives!

Language Arts

Because the language arts include listening, speaking, reading, and writing, this content area is an intrinsic part of everyone's life. It is about communication, both imparted and received. It is tied to linguistic intelligence (Gardner, 1993), which our society values greatly. And it is part of every curriculum, in one form or another, from preschool through advanced education.

Movement and literacy have a great deal in common. Like language, movement is a form of communication and self-expression. Body language is a distinct method of communicating. Many believe that "ideas and feelings expressed in words actually begin in the body. . . . Before you write or speak, there is a physical response in the body" (Minton, 2003, p. 37). There is also evidence that during communication, the body expresses more than words do. For example, if you instruct a group of people to put their hands over their eyes, while simultaneously placing your own hands over your *ears*, the vast majority will mimic your *action* rather than respond to your words.

Rhythm is also an essential component of both movement and the language arts. As children acquire and refine their motor skills, they learn subconscious lessons about rhythm. For instance, a gallop matches a 2/4 musical meter, a walk is similar to a 4/4 meter, and a skip has the feel of a 6/8. And people have personal rhythms for thinking and moving. For example, when you ask children to get into a small body shape, they all respond at their own pace, some quickly and some more slowly. And because words and sentences have rhythms—and we develop an internal rhythm when reading and writing—movement experiences help create an awareness of the rhythm of literary works and help children "internalize the beat" when they're reading and writing (Block, 2001, p. 44).

Similarly, when children string movements together to form sequences and eventually dances, gymnastic routines, or sport actions, it's similar to the linking of words to form sentences and eventually paragraphs. Both require that children choose components that naturally flow. Both require breathing room (a pause in the action or a comma) and, finally, an ending (a full stop or a period). Thus, the movement element of flow—free and bound—is also relevant to emergent literacy.

Consider prepositions, those little words so critical to language and life. As children move over, under, around, through, beside, and near objects and others—for example, *under* a partner's legs, *through* the hoop, *over* the balance beam—these words take on greater significance than they do in a traditional grammar lesson (see figure 7.1).

Figure 7.1 Crawling *through* and *under* teaches lessons about prepositions.

Spatial orientation is necessary for letter identification and the orientation of symbols on a page (Olds, 1994). For example, a lowercase "b" and a lowercase "d" are the same; both are composed of a line and a circle. The only difference is in their spatial orientation—which side of the line the circle is on. When children take on the straight and curving lines of letters with their bodies and body parts, rather than simply attempting to copy them from a chart on the wall, their senses of directionality and spatial orientation are greatly enhanced.

When your students perform a slow walk or they skip lightly, adjectives and adverbs become much more than abstract concepts. When they're given the opportunity to physically demonstrate such action words as *stomp, pounce, stalk,* or *slither* or descriptive words like *smooth, gentle,* or *enormous,* word comprehension is immediate and long lasting.

When children speak and listen to one another, as when they solve movement problems cooperatively, they're using and expanding their vocabularies and learning important lessons in communication. When they invent rules for games, as young children like to do, they further enhance their communication skills and make essential connections among the physical, social-emotional, and cognitive domains.

Remember, too, that activities that strengthen children's hands, like climbing and hanging and swinging, benefit their ability to write as well

! TRY THIS

- In addition to forming letter shapes alone and with partners, the children can gain additional experience with the shapes of letters by "writing" them in the air in front of them with ribbon sticks (pretending the ribbon sticks are chalk and the air is a chalkboard). Begin by inviting them to make each letter you assign as large as possible. Eventually they can make them smaller and smaller.

- Challenge the children to form the shape of letters you assign or of the letter that begins their first name, if they're ready for this, with a jump rope on the floor. Ask them to trace the pathway created by this shape with various locomotor skills. For example, you might invite them first to walk along the shape of each letter. Later, you could ask them to jump or gallop.

- To help children feel comfortable moving in a top-to-bottom direction, which is necessary for reading and writing, challenge them to practice movements that take them in those directions. For example, move body parts (one or both hands, a nose, a shoulder) or the whole body from up high to down low.

- To combine top-to-bottom spatial orientation with word comprehension, invite the children to show you the differences among words like *shrink, melt, collapse,* and *shrivel*. This activity is most appropriate for early elementary children and may require your assistance.

- Walking, jumping, and hopping sideward from left to right provides practice with left-to-right directionality, as does sliding left to right. In a society in which reading and writing occur in this direction, such activities are invaluable.

as their physical development. Also, cross-lateral movement, like swinging a ribbon stick across the body or slithering, prompts the two hemispheres of the brain to communicate across the corpus callosum. This also benefits children's reading and writing abilities (Hannaford, 2005).

Mathematics

At first it may seem that the only thing movement and math have in common is beginning with the letter "m." However, that may be a result of thinking about math in the "adult" way, remembering formal school experiences involving algebra, calculus, or trigonometry. But if you look at math concepts that are developmentally appropriate for exploration with children ages four to eight, you'll see several correlations between math and movement.

For example, quantitative concepts are an important part of the language of early mathematics. Physical educators can see significant overlap between their subject and these concepts. Students moving through the levels in space will concurrently experience *big* and *little, high* and *low,* and *tall* and *short.* Students working on the movement element of force will physically experience *light* and *heavy.* When they practice jumping forward, they can make attempts for *longer* jumps and then the *longest* jump of all. When students work together in *pairs* or *groups;* when they form lines, with someone *first, last,* and in the *middle;* and when they perform a movement *once* or *twice more,* they experience math. These experiences also enhance word comprehension, which is critical to emergent literacy.

Mayesky (2006) believes the following quantitative concepts should be part of the daily routines of young children:

• Big and little	• Few	• Bunch
• Long and short	• Tall and short	• Group
• High and low	• Light and heavy	• Pair
• Wide and narrow	• Together	• Many
• Late and early	• Same length	• More
• First and last	• Highest	• Most
• Middle	• Lowest	• Twice
• Once	• Longer than	

Time is one of the cognitive concepts that contribute to the gradual acquisition of mathematics knowledge (Essa, 2007). Therefore, when children explore the movement element of time—moving very slowly and very quickly and at speeds in between—the concept of time is not abstract but concrete. Concurrently, abstract words such as *slow* and *fast* take on much more meaning than if they were merely part of a vocabulary list.

Shape, too, is part of both math and PE. Geometry in the early years begins with an understanding of lines—vertical, horizontal, diagonal, and crossed—all of which children in PE class will make with their bodies and body parts. Your students likely are not yet ready to consider acute and obtuse angles, but they can create them with their elbows and knees by creating crooked or pointy shapes (see figure 7.2). And when body parts connect, students can form circles, squares, and triangles, among other shapes, which correlates with exploration of the movement element of shape.

Clapping or stepping while counting to the beat of the music reinforces counting, one-to-one correspondence, and patterning, all critical to early mathematics. Similarly, the child happily moving to or accompanying a polka, in a 2/4 meter, or a waltz, in a 3/4 meter, with a ribbon stick is gaining another

! TRY THIS

Playing the Shadow Game, in which one partner leads and the other shadows, offers an opportunity for children to experience the concepts of *in front of* and *behind* while practicing a variety of locomotor skills. Be sure to suggest that they vary their pathways, tempo, body shape, amount of force, levels, and so forth.

experience in patterning, while also getting the *feel* of fractions.

To promote number recognition, challenge the children to form the shapes of numbers with their bodies or body parts. To begin, assign numbers they must replicate, inviting them to try at various levels: standing, kneeling, sitting, and lying. When the children are developmentally ready, ask them to choose numbers, say, between zero and four, or five and nine.

Figure 7.2 A student creates angles with his elbows and knees.

Here are other ideas for combining math and PE:

- Challenge students to show you their ages with their bodies or to form numbers in pairs or trios.

- Invite students to form the shapes of numbers with jump ropes and to trace the pathways created by those shapes with locomotor skills.

- Help your students practice their counting skills by counting beats clapped or steps taken, for example, giving the class a number and asking the children to take that many steps or hop that many hops. Or ask them to count the repetitions performed; for example, ask the children to repeat a movement two more times.

- Invite the children to discover how many ways they can move an arm, a leg, the head, a hand, or a shoulder.

- Ask your students to place a certain number of body parts on the floor or to balance on a certain number of parts. More challenging, and involving simple computation, is an extension of this activity in which you ask the children to add or subtract a certain number of parts to or from those already touching the floor. For instance, begin by asking the children to put three body parts on the floor. Once they've accomplished this, challenge them to add or subtract one body part. How many parts are now touching the floor?

Science

The word *science* may remind you of topics such as chemistry, physics, biology, botany, and astronomy. You may imagine men and women in lab coats, poring over facts and figures or measuring strange concoctions into test tubes and beakers. Because none of this is relevant in the lives of young children, you might wonder—rightly—how science fits into the early childhood or physical education curriculum.

Well, science is also about exploration, investigation, problem solving, and discovery, all of which *are* relevant for young children and also should be part of a child's early physical education experiences. The principal difference between these two views of science is that much of the "lab coat" view deals with the theoretical and the abstract, while exploration and problem solving, as far as young children are concerned, deal with the concrete and the tangible, what can be easily observed. In other words, science for young children is learning by doing, just as movement is.

Many themes typically explored in early childhood classrooms fall under the science category, including the human body: identifying body parts and their functions, the senses, hygiene, and nutrition. Body-part identification, with activities like Simon Says and Head, Shoulders, Knees, and Toes, is therefore where the connection between movement and science begins for young children.

Of course, any time children move, they're learning something about the functions—the capabilities and limitations—of the human body and its parts. However, you can be more specific by focusing on certain functions. Ask your students to concentrate on the muscles, for example, by suggesting that they think about the amount of muscle tension used to perform a movement or the shape of the muscles when they freeze in different positions. Relaxation exercises that require the children to contract and relax the muscles (like Statues and Rag Dolls, page 39) are also excellent for developing an awareness of these important body parts. Similarly, relaxation exercises focusing on breathing can create an awareness of the lungs.

Introduce the function of the heart by asking children to feel their pulse at rest and after vigorous activity. Challenge them to match their pulse's rhythm by tapping a hand or foot. Listening activities like Statues, described in chapter 3 (page 39), focus on the sense of hearing. Asking children to try various nonlocomotor movement with their eyes closed draws attention to the sense of sight, as does Sitting in the Dark, described in chapter 4 (page 56).

Moving like animals, another theme that falls under the content area of science, is relevant to young children because they find animals so appealing. It also offers a great opportunity for exploring various movement skills and elements. It's not enough, however, to merely ask the children

! TRY THIS

- Asking students to alternately pretend to be robots made completely of metal and then astronauts floating weightlessly in space calls attention to the muscles and the movement element of force. The element of flow is also involved here because being a robot is an example of bound flow, while floating weightlessly is an example of free flow.

- When children pretend to be balloons slowly inflating by starting small and gradually expanding as they breathe in through the nose and deflating by getting smaller as they breathe out through the mouth, they're gaining experience with the functions of the lungs.

to pretend to be different animals. You should create a greater awareness by discussing pertinent characteristics of the animals they portray. Cats, for example, can move slowly and quietly. What is it about the way they use their muscles and paws that makes this possible? What is it about their spines that makes them able to twist, stretch, and arch so easily?

Alternately pretending to be cats then elephants provides experience with the movement element of force as well as the mathematics concepts of size and *light* and *heavy*. The same can be said when children alternately pretend to move like rabbits then kangaroos, which is also a fun way for young children to practice jumping.

Of course, there are specific scientific concepts that are developmentally appropriate for exploration and which contribute to the children's physical education. To explore the scientific concept of flotation, for instance, children can watch bubbles, feathers, or chiffon scarves drift through the air and then attempt to simulate the movement. Does floating require light or strong movement? Little or great muscle tension? Is it possible for human beings to really float? No, because of *gravity*. When we jump, hop, or leap into the air, the force of gravity pulls us back down just as it pulls down any object, such as a beanbag or a ball, we toss into the air. But the higher we toss the object, the longer it takes it to reach the ground. Challenge the children to discover how many times they can clap or turn around before the beanbag or scarf returns to their hands or to the ground. Which object offers the opportunity for more claps or turns? Why do they think this is?

Gravity is also a factor when we attempt to balance. Invite the children to balance on their knees or seat, lean in any direction as far as they can before falling over, and then return to their original positions. This is

❗ TRY THIS

Appropriate for early elementary children is experience with the concept of counterbalance. Invite partners to link hands and lean as far away from each other as they can without stumbling or falling. Ask them to put their palms together and find a way to balance by pushing against each other.

called balance and recovery. Now ask them to lean again, this time going beyond the point of recovery. What happens? Gravity causes them to fall over. You can also help your students discover that balance is easier when the body's center of gravity is lowered and there's a large, rather than a narrow, base of support.

Other scientific concepts may be less obvious candidates for movement exploration, but that doesn't mean movement can't be used or that movement can't make these ideas less abstract. Rowen (1982) suggests the children discover action and reaction (every action force has an equal and opposite reaction force) by sitting on the floor in pairs with legs straddled, feet touching, and hands held. As one child pushes forward *slowly,* the other pulls back. Then they reverse. This also contributes to muscle strength and endurance.

Additionally, children are familiar with most, if not all, of the six simple machines: lever, wheel, pulley, inclined plane, screw, and wedge. They can roll like wheels and twist like screwdrivers, and in your gym they may have access to inclined planes and wedges meant specifically for movement.

Appropriate for early elementary children is a game called The Machine, which not only begins to develop the children's understanding of machinery but also is an excellent exercise in cooperation that provides practice with nonlocomotor movement. In this activity, one child begins by repeatedly performing a movement that can be executed in place. A second child then stands near the first and contributes a second movement that relates in some way to the first. For example, if the first child is performing an up–down motion by bending and straightening the knees, the second child might choose to do the reverse, standing beside his or her classmate. A third child might choose an arm or leg motion timed to move between the two bodies moving up and down. As these movements continue, each remaining student adds a functioning part to the machine. Students may choose any movements, as long as they don't interfere with the actions of others and they contribute in some way to the machine. Once all the parts are functioning, you can ask each child to make a sound that represents his or her part.

Social Studies

Lessons in social studies for young children begin with the children themselves, because that's where their world begins. Self-concept, therefore, is a logical starting point in the early childhood social studies curriculum. The child's world then extends, progressively, to family, friends, neighborhood, and the larger community. In early childhood settings, these topics generally fall under the themes of self-awareness, families and friends, holidays and celebrations, transportation, and multicultural education and diversity.

Emotion is one aspect of self-awareness that fits better under social studies than under science. If a young child is to have a positive self-concept, he needs to accept his feelings as a part of himself to later gain greater understanding of them. He must also learn that others have feelings, too. Activities in which children pretend to walk as though sad, mad, proud, scared, tired, or happy are a good place to start because they give children permission to express themselves and a safe place in which to do it. An exercise like this also gives children a fun way to explore a simple locomotor skill like walking.

 TRY THIS

For a cool-down or a warm-up, ask the students to show you how their faces or hands would look if they were frightened, sad, mad, or happy.

The concept of friends is best explored in the gym via cooperative activities. Cooperation is a social skill that must be *learned*. Although society and many PE programs place more value on competition than on cooperation, preschoolers who are given a choice prefer cooperation. Also, what most people fail to realize is that, developmentally speaking, children must first learn to cooperate before they can successfully compete.

When children are given the chance to work together toward a solution or common goal—whether creating a game or a group shape—they know they each contribute to the success of the venture. Each child realizes he or she plays a vital role in the outcome, and each accepts the responsibility of fulfilling that role. They also learn to become tolerant of others' ideas and to accept the similarities and differences of other children. Furthermore, cooperative activities seldom cause the feelings of inferiority that can result from the comparisons made during competition. On the contrary, because cooperative and noncompetitive activities lead to a greater chance for success, they generate greater confidence in children.

The following cooperative games foster body and spatial awareness, problem solving, teamwork, and other educational lessons:

• Group Balance. The children form a standing circle and place their hands on the shoulders of the children on either side of them. They must then maintain a steady balance through challenges to stand on one foot; lean forward, backward, left, and right; rise onto tiptoes; and so on.

• Musical Hoops. Scatter hoops throughout the gym and instruct the children to each stand inside one. When you start playing music, the children leave their hoops and walk around the gym. As the children are walking, remove one of the hoops. When the music stops, the children step inside the closest hoop, sharing the ones remaining. Begin another round, assigning a different locomotor skill if you want, once more removing a hoop. Continue the game until just one hoop remains, which the children must determine how to share. Hint: Even if everyone gets just a big toe inside the hoop, they have met your challenge.

• It Takes Two. This activity requires partners to connect various body parts: matching parts, such as right hands, left elbows, or right feet or nonmatching parts, such as a hand and an elbow, an elbow and a shoulder, or a wrist and a hip. The objectives of the game are to stay connected and to discover how many ways it's possible to move while remaining connected.

• Footsie Rolls. Once your students are able to execute log rolls on their own, they can try it in pairs. Partners lie on their backs with the soles of their feet together. They then see how far they can roll without their feet breaking contact.

Transportation, of course, is a social studies theme that lends itself readily to movement. To make problem solving part of your exercises, ask children to think of and depict modes of transportation found mainly in cities, on water, and in the sky or transportation that doesn't use motors. You can introduce the children to traffic lights by playing a movement game with three sheets of paper: one red, one yellow, and one green. When you hold up the green sheet, the children walk. They walk in place when they see the yellow sheet and come to a complete stop when you hold up the red. Once they're familiar with this game, use it to provide practice with other locomotor skills.

To explore diversity, introduce the children's games, songs, and dances of a variety of cultures. Children's recordings of multicultural music are plentiful. Remember, too, that you can find collections of folk songs at the library that aren't specifically intended for children but are still suitable for movement activities.

Art

Art and movement have many things in common, particularly where young children are concerned. Art, because it involves movement, helps develop motor skills. Gross motor skills are used in art activities such as painting on an easel, creating murals, body tracing, and working with clay. Fine motor control, which is refined later than gross motor control, is practiced during art activities such as working with small paintbrushes, cutting with scissors, and pasting. Both art and movement also help develop eye–hand coordination.

Additionally, art and movement both encourage self-expression. When given ample opportunity to explore possibilities, whether through movement or a variety of art materials, children make nonverbal statements about who they are and what is important to them. Through both media, they can express emotions and work out issues of concern to them and achieve the satisfaction that comes from experiencing success. However, these results can occur only when the child's movement responses and artwork are free from adult censorship and when they're accepted and valued as evidence of the child's individuality. With acceptance, children gain confidence in their abilities to express themselves, solve problems, and use their creativity.

Finally, concepts like shape, size, spatial relationships, and line are part of both art and physical education. Whenever children arrange their bodies in the space around them, it can be said they're exploring artistic concepts as well as physical ones. With their bodies, they're creating lines and shapes. When they move to different levels, in different directions, along different pathways and in relation to others and to objects, they're increasing their spatial awareness. But even the abstract artistic concepts of color and texture can be explored and expressed through movement.

To explore shape with the youngest children, offer simple comparisons between straight and round. Show the children straight and round objects and ask them to create these opposite shapes with their bodies or body parts.

Later, you can ask them to form bridges and tunnels with their bodies or body parts. This is an excellent way to promote flexibility. More advanced activities, which, incidentally, overlap with the content area of mathematics, include challenging the children to show you pointed, angular, and oval shapes and to explore the possibilities for symmetrical and asymmetrical shapes. You'll find other suggestions for exploring shape in chapter 3.

Color and shape can be explored in tandem by providing pictures or examples of objects in various colors, for example, a yellow banana, a red apple, or a green plant, and asking the children to demonstrate the shape of each object (see figure 7.3). An alternative is to mention a color and ask the children what it brings to mind. They can then either take on the shapes of the objects mentioned or interpret them. For instance, if the color green reminds some children of frogs, they could depict the movement of frogs. If the color blue reminds children of the ocean, they might depict swimming.

Figure 7.3   "Show me the shape of a banana."

You can explore primary colors with your students by forming three groups and assigning each a primary color. To begin, the children depict or take on the shape of everything they can think of in their assigned color. The children then begin mixing. For example, when a child from the red group joins a child from the blue group, they depict or take on the shape of *purple* things. When a child from the yellow group joins a child from the red group, they depict *orange* things.

To focus on the concept of lines, use a jump rope to demonstrate the differences among vertical, horizontal, diagonal, curved, and crooked lines. Invite the children to use their bodies to replicate the line you've created with the rope. An activity like this not only promotes understanding of this artistic element, but it also contributes to your students' body and spatial awareness and is part of introductory geometry, which falls under mathematics.

For the concept of texture, gather items of various textures for the children to see and feel, for example, a rope, a beach ball, a chiffon scarf, and a feather. Talk to them about how each item feels or *makes them feel*. For instance, a feather might make them feel ticklish. Then ask them to demonstrate this feeling through movement. An activity like this may not directly contribute to motor skill development or fitness, but it definitely enhances self-expression. And an individual who feels comfortable with physical self-expression is one who will likely feel comfortable with movement itself, which *will* contribute to motor skill development and fitness.

Music

It's impossible to think of music and movement as separate entities when young children are involved. For them, experiencing music isn't limited to the auditory sense, as evidenced by even an infant's whole-body response to it.

Songs, movement, and musical games are "brilliant neurological exercises" vital to intellectual development (Coulter, 1995, p. 22). Coulter states that by combining rhythmic movement with speech and song, young children are given an opportunity to further develop their minds, particularly in the areas of inner speech and impulse control, which contribute to language development, self-management, and social skills. A great deal of evidence also shows that music activities engage the left, right, front, and back portions of the brain. In fact, studying music involves more right- and left-brain functions than any other activity measured (Habermeyer, 1999).

All of this adds up to a great deal of rationale for including music as part of your curriculum. But, as pointed out in chapter 3, music contributes not only to the child's development and general education but also to the child's *physical* education. And it can contribute to your program, sparking new ideas, generating enthusiasm, and helping to either energize or soothe.

Running, for example, can be much more fun when performed to the accompaniment of a song with a running rhythm, like "Chariots of Fire." A game of Statues, in which the children move while the music is playing and freeze when you hit the pause button, gives children the incentive and freedom to experiment with movement improvisation. It also helps children learn to differentiate between sound and silence and to practice stopping and starting. And a cool-down at the end of your lesson can certainly be aided by a piece of relaxing music, like a George Winston piano solo or Pachelbel's *Canon in D-Major*. All of these are examples of the ways in which your students can learn concepts important to both music and physical education at the same time.

 TRY THIS

- To explore bound flow (interrupted movement) with your students, play a recording of or sing "Pop Goes the Weasel." Instruct the children to walk around the gym until they hear the "pop," at which time they're to jump into the air and then continue walking. Eventually you can challenge the children to jump and change direction at the pop.

- To explore levels in space, use a slide whistle (or hum or intone), moving from low notes to high notes and back again as the children move from low to high positions and back again. With your youngest students, you may first want to ask them to experience this with their arms alone.

- A fun way to explore rhythm is with body sounds. Challenge the children to discover at least two different sounds they can create with their hands. Then ask them what other body parts they can use to create sound. (Possibilities include feet, tongue, and teeth.) Ask them to move around the gym accompanying themselves with some of these sounds.

Making the Links Stronger

Following are simple steps you can take to further enhance students' learning and strengthen the connections between your gym and the classroom.

- Put words to the students' actions. When your students move through the levels in space, say aloud the words *high, low,* and in the *middle.* When the students form lines, use the words *first, last,* and in the *middle.* When they form straight lines with their bodies while standing or lying, they should hear the words *vertical* and *horizontal,* respectively. And when they explore straight and round shapes with their bodies, point out the lines and circles they've created to acknowledge and reinforce their understanding.

- Invite students to use words. When the children label their own actions, positions, and shapes, they must find and use the correct terms. This adds another sense to the learning process and helps the children make important connections.

- Post signs. To create more sensory input, post signs around the gym. Display lines, simple geometric shapes, and directions in both picture and word form. For example, label a vertical line with an arrow at both the top and bottom as *up* and *down*. A horizontal line with arrows at either end represents *left* and *right*. Not only is this helpful to the children on multiple levels, but it also lets classroom teachers and administrators see how connections are being made.

Aristotle said, "What we have to learn, we learn by doing." Confucius concurred. He said, "What I hear, I forget. What I see, I remember. What I do, I know." With a bit of extra verbal and visual aid, as your young students acquire, modify, and master movement skills in your gym, they will become physically educated people who both *do* and *know*.

REMEMBER THIS

As you can see, it isn't necessary to invent connections among physical education and the other content areas; they occur naturally (see table 7.1). And because active learning is superior to the passive reception of information, PE teachers have much in their favor. Of course, the PE teacher shouldn't remain the only person aware of these connections. It's helpful to develop a reciprocal relationship between the gym and the classroom so that everyone knows what the students are working on and to effectively promote the links between the two areas.

Table 7.1   Links Between PE and Content Areas

PE component	Content area
Element of space	Art, language arts
Element of shape	Art, math, language arts
Element of time	Math, science
Element of force	Math, science
Element of flow	Language arts, music, science
Element of rhythm	Language arts, music
Body-part identification	Science
Self-expression	Art, social studies
Cooperative activities	Social studies
Fine motor control	Language arts

- Children who engage in physical activity demonstrate improved academic performance, higher test scores, and a better attitude toward school.
- More of the brain is activated during physical activity than during seatwork.
- Children learn best through active involvement, using as many senses as possible.
- When using movement across the curriculum, you can help make the connections stronger by putting words to the students' actions, inviting the students to use words themselves, and posting signs.

Appendix A

Sample Lesson Plans

Following are three sample lesson plans: one for ages four to five, the second for ages five to six, and the third for ages six through eight. Each includes activities you've seen in the book, arranged here to give you an example of how you can use them to create a lesson plan. These sample lessons include two warm-up activities, one of which involves exploring an element of movement; two or more fitness activities, including one that involves flexibility and one that involves motor skill development; and two cool-down activities. Each lesson consists of at least six activities, which should be sufficient to cover approximately 45 minutes of class time. This will vary, of course, depending on the size, age, and experience of your groups.

LESSON PLAN 1: AGES FOUR TO FIVE

Warm-Up Activity 1: *Inside My Bubble*

Objectives   Warm-up, awareness of personal space
Equipment   One poly spot, carpet square, or hoop per student
                    See chapter 3, page 33.

Warm-Up Activity 2: *Head, Belly, Toes*

Objectives   Warm-up, body-part identification, flexibility
Equipment   None
                    See chapter 2, page 13.

Fitness Activity 1: *Rabbits and 'Roos*

Objectives   Muscular strength and endurance (fitness components),
                    practice with jumping (motor skill development)
Equipment   None
                    See chapter 5, page 72.

Fitness Activity 2: *Stretch and Bend*

Objectives   Flexibility (fitness), awareness of personal space
Equipment   None
                    See chapter 4, page 55.

Cool-Down Activity 1: *Statues and Rag Dolls*

Objectives   Cool-down, practice with relaxation, awareness of muscles,
                    introduction to the element of force
Equipment   None
                    See chapter 3, page 39.

Cool-Down Activity 2: *"Where Is Thumbkin?"*

Objectives   Cool-down, body-part identification, development of fine
                    motor coordination
Equipment   None
                    See chapter 6, page 81.

Warm-Up Activity 1: *Body Poem*

Objectives Warm-up, body-part identification

Equipment None
　　　　　　See chapter 2, page 14.

Warm-Up Activity 2: *Exploring Force*

Objectives Warm-up, awareness of muscles, experience with elements
　　　　　　of force and flow

Equipment None
　　　　　　See chapter 3, page 39.

Fitness Activity 1: *Gallop!*

Objectives Practice with galloping (motor skill development), experi-
　　　　　　ence with personal and general space

Equipment Piece of music with a 2/4 meter, or hand drum and mallet
　　　　　　(optional)
　　　　　　See chapter 4, page 52.

Fitness Activity 2: *Statues*

Objectives Cardiorespiratory endurance (fitness), self-expression, prac-
　　　　　　tice stopping and starting, differentiating between sound and
　　　　　　silence

Equipment Recordings of moderate- to fast-paced music
　　　　　　See chapter 3, page 39.

Fitness Activity 3: *Bridges and Tunnels*

Objectives Flexibility (fitness), cooperation

Equipment None
　　　　　　See chapter 5, page 74.

Cool-Down Activity 1: *I'm Melting!*

Objectives Cool-down, practice with relaxation, practice with slow
　　　　　　movement

Equipment None
　　　　　　See chapter 2, page 27.

Cool-Down Activity 2: *Opening and Closing Fingers*

Objectives Cool-down, development of fine motor control

Equipment None
　　　　　　See chapter 6, page 81.

LESSON PLAN 3: AGES SIX TO EIGHT

Warm-Up Activity 1: *Simon Says*

Objectives   Warm-up, body-part identification, promotion of listening skills

Equipment   None
See chapter 2, page 13.

Warm-Up Activity 2: *Shrinking Room*

Objectives   Warm-up, experience with personal and general space

Equipment   None
See chapter 3, page 34.

Fitness Activity 1: *Group Slide*

Objective   Practice with sliding (motor skill development)

Equipment   None
See chapter 4, page 53.

Fitness Activity 2: *"Beep Beep"*

Objectives   Cardiorespiratory endurance (fitness), practice physically imitating what the eyes see, experience with the concept of accelerando

Equipment   Recording of "Beep Beep"
See chapter 3, page 38.

Cool-Down Activity 1: *Exploring Bending and Stretching*

Objectives   Cool-down, flexibility (fitness)

Equipment   None
See chapter 4, page 55.

Cool-Down Activity 2: *Slo-Mo*

Objectives   Cool-down, practice with slow movement

Equipment   None
See chapter 3, page 38.

Appendix B

Resources

Children's Music

Educational Activities, Inc.
P.O. Box 87
Baldwin, NY 11510
800-797-3223
www.edact.com

Educational Record Center
3233 Burnt Mill Dr., Suite 100
Wilmington, NC 28403
888-372-4543
www.erckids.com

Kimbo Educational
P.O. Box 477
Long Branch, NJ 07740
800-631-2187
www.kimboed.com

Melody House
819 N.W. 92nd St.
Oklahoma City, OK 73114
800-234-9228
www.melodyhousemusic.com

Equipment and Props

Flaghouse
601 Flaghouse Dr.
Hasbrouck Heights, NJ 07604
800-793-7900
www.flaghouse.com

Play With a Purpose
P.O. Box 998
Owatonna, MN 55060
888-330-1826
www.pwaponline.com

Sportime
P.O. Box 922668
Norcross, GA 30010
800-283-5700
www.sportime.com

Professional Organizations

American Academy of Pediatrics
141 N.W. Point Blvd.
Elk Grove Village, IL 60007
847-434-4000
www.aap.org

The AAP is an organization of 60,000 pediatricians dedicated to the physical, mental, and social health of infants, children, adolescents, and young adults. Resources include fact sheets relative to topics such as childhood obesity and policy statements on topics such as young children and sport participation.

American Alliance for Health, Physical Education, Recreation and Dance
1900 Association Dr.
Reston, VA 20191
800-213-7193
www.aahperd.org

AAHPERD is an alliance of five national associations, six district associations, and a research consortium that support healthy lifestyles through high-quality programs. Among the national associations are the National Association for Sport and Physical Education (NASPE) and the American Association for Health Education (AAHE). Resources include books for PE and health professionals, policy statements, standards for physical education, and an annual conference.

Early Childhood Music and Movement Association
805 Mill Ave.
Snohomish, WA 98290
360-568-5635
www.ecmma.org

The ECMMA is a professional organization that supports the field of early childhood music and movement through education, advocacy, and networking. As teachers of young children in myriad settings, members benefit from attending national conventions, regional conferences, and local chapter gatherings that sponsor innovative leaders and their work in their profession. Because ECMMA is a nonprofit organization, it is uniquely qualified to provide a forum for research and teaching for all early childhood educators, therapists, and academics.

National Association for the Education of Young Children
1313 L St. N.W., Suite 500
Washington, DC 20005
800-424-2460
www.naeyc.org

NAEYC is dedicated to improving the well-being of all young children, with particular focus on the quality of educational and developmental services for children from birth through age eight. NAEYC is the world's largest organization working on behalf of young children, with nearly 100,000 members, a national network of more than 300 local, state, and regional affiliates, and a growing global alliance of like-minded organizations. Membership is open to everyone who shares a desire to serve and act on behalf of the needs and rights of all young children. Resources include the journal, *Young Children;* books; policy statements; and an annual conference.

President's Council on Physical Fitness and Sports
Department W
200 Independence Ave., S.W., Room 738-H
Washington, DC 20201
202-690-9000
www.fitness.gov

The President's Council on Physical Fitness and Sports is an advisory committee of volunteer citizens who advise the president through the secretary of health and human services about physical activity, fitness, and sports in America. Through its programs and partnerships with the public, private, and nonprofit sectors, the council serves as a catalyst to promote health, physical activity, fitness, and enjoyment for people of all ages, backgrounds, and abilities through participation in physical activity and sport. The 20 council members are appointed and serve at the pleasure of the president.

Web Sites Offering Research and Resources

American Association for the Child's Right to Play
www.ipausa.org

IPA/USA is the national affiliate of the International Play Association. Its purpose is to protect, preserve, and promote play as a fundamental right for all humans. As such, the organization is a leading advocate for recess. The IPA/USA Web site offers research on the importance of recess as well as the importance of physical activity in general.

Body, Mind and Child Radio
www.bodymindandchild.com/radio.htm

Body, Mind and Child Radio offers 10- to 12-minute podcasts exploring topics such as the need for physical education, the connection between mind and body, the worldwide childhood obesity crisis, and children's involvement in sports. Primarily intended for the parents of children up to age eight, the information shared by guests in the fields of early childhood education, motor development, the neurosciences, and more can be used as an advocacy tool.

Human Kinetics
www.HumanKinetics.com

Human Kinetics is the world's largest provider of information related to physical activity. Offering books, journals, online courses, software, and audiovisual products, HK is committed to providing high-quality informational and educational products in the physical activity and health fields.

Moving and Learning
www.movingandlearning.com

This site offers articles, activities, and resources devoted to physical education and physical activity for children from birth to age eight.

PE Central
www.pecentral.com

PE Central is the premier Web site for health and physical education teachers, parents, and students. The site's goal is to provide the latest information about developmentally appropriate physical education programs for children and youth. The site offers numerous resources, including best-practice ideas, lesson plans, and a job center.

Rescuing Recess
www.rescuingrecess.com

The Cartoon Network has created a national movement to safeguard and promote daily recess. The initial effort helped more than 5 million students in 15 percent of U.S. schools get outside and get moving. More than 10,000 free "Rescuing Recess" kits, with playground equipment, activity ideas, and games, were distributed to schools in all 50 states to help start and maintain a recess monitor program. Elementary schools in more than 4,600 cities hosted recess rallies, made possible by volunteer parents, educators, and community members. More than 104,000 letters were sent to state education policy makers.

Glossary

body composition—The body's makeup in terms of the percentage of fat, muscle, tissue, and bone, or the ratio of lean body tissue to fat.

cardiorespiratory endurance—The ability of the heart and lungs to supply oxygen and nutrients to the muscles.

cognitive domain—The developmental realm related to intellectual growth.

convergent problem solving—A teaching method, also known as guided discovery, in which the teacher has a specific task or concept in mind (e.g., teaching children to perform a step-hop, or that a wide base of support provides the most stable balance). Teachers then lead students through a sequence of questions and challenges toward discovery of the task or concept. This process, although still allowing for inventiveness and experimentation, guides the children as they *converge* on the right answer.

depth perception—The ability to judge distance in relation to oneself.

direct approach—A command style of teaching that uses demonstration and imitation.

divergent problem solving—A style of teaching, also known as movement exploration, in which any single challenge can have several correct responses.

elements of movement—Variations that describe *how* a movement is performed. If we liken movement education to the study of grammar, the skills themselves can be considered *verbs* and the six movement elements—space, shape, time, force, flow, and rhythm—are the *adverbs* modifying them.

figure–ground perception—The ability to separate or distinguish an object from its surroundings.

fine motor skills—Movement of the small muscles controlling the hands, fingers, and thumb in coordination with the eyes.

fingerplays—Poems or word plays in which movement—traditionally of the hands and fingers—has an important function.

flexibility—The range of motion around joints.

flow—An element of movement. Bound flow is halting or punctuated movement. Free flow is uninterrupted movement.

force—The element of movement related to the lightness or heaviness of a movement. Also refers to the degree of muscle tension involved.

general space—Physical area normally limited only by walls, floors, and ceilings. May also be referred to as shared space.

gross motor skills—Movements using the large muscles of the body.

guided discovery—A teaching method using convergent problem solving.

health-related fitness—The component of physical fitness that consists of cardiorespiratory endurance, muscular strength, muscular endurance, flexibility, and body composition.

locomotor skills—Movements that transport the body as a whole from one point to another. Examples include walking, running, and galloping.

manipulative skills—A gross motor skill that usually involves an object being manipulated. Traditional manipulative skills are those typically related to sport and game playing (e.g., throwing and catching). Nontraditional manipulative skills are those with which young children already have experience (e.g., pulling and pushing).

movement exploration—A teaching method also known as divergent problem solving.

muscular endurance—The muscles' ability to continue contracting over an extended period of time. It is related to stamina.

muscular strength—The ability to exert force with a single maximum effort.

nonlocomotor skills—Movements performed in place, usually while standing, kneeling, sitting, or lying. Sometimes called axial movements, they involve the axis of the body rotating around a fixed point.

peripheral vision—The ability to see things to the side while the eyes are focused on a central point.

personal space—The area immediately surrounding the body.

physical domain—The developmental realm related to physical growth.

rhythm—The movement element related to music. It also encompasses the many rhythms of life. Words, for instance, have rhythm, as do the various locomotor skills (e.g., the rhythm of a hop is different from that of a gallop). People, in fact, possess their own personal rhythms for both thinking and functioning.

shape—The element of movement related to the various forms the body can assume.

skill-related fitness—The component of physical fitness that incorporates balance, agility, coordination, power, speed, and reaction time.

social-emotional domain—The developmental realm that begins with self-discovery and results in the ability to interact with others. It is also referred to as affective development.

time—The element of movement related to how slowly or quickly a movement is performed.

visual–motor coordination—The ability to integrate the use of the eyes and hands in terms of object tracking.

References

Activity and Health Research. 1992. *Allied Dunbar national fitness survey.* London: Sports Council and Health Education Authority.

American Academy of Pediatrics. 1992. Fitness, activity, and sports participation in the preschool child. *Pediatrics* 90: 1002-1004.

American Academy of Pediatrics. 2001. Strength training by children and adolescents. *Pediatrics* 107(6): 1470-1472.

Bach, G. 1997. Start smart. *Parks & Recreation* 32(4): 106-110.

Block, B.A. 2001. Literacy through movement: An organizational approach. *Journal of Physical Education, Recreation, and Dance* 72(1): 39-48.

Burnett, D.J. 2001. *It's just a game!* San Jose, CA: Authors Choice Press.

Buschner, C.A. 1990. Can we help children move and think critically? In *Moving and learning for the young child* (pp. 73-76), edited by W.J. Stinson. Reston, VA: AAHPERD.

Charlesworth, R. 2008. *Understanding child development.* Clifton Park, NY: Delmar Learning.

Colman, A. 1996. Skills appalling. *Youth Studies* 15(1): 1-7.

Cooper, K. 1999. *FitKids.* Nashville: Broadman & Holman.

Coulter, D. 1995. Music and the making of the mind. *Early Childhood Connections: The Journal of Music- and Movement-Based Learning* 1: 22-26.

Dolgoff, S. n.d. Will your child get an eating disorder? When a preschooler believes thin is in, there may be trouble ahead. www.sesameworkshop.org/parents/advice/article.php?contentId=7516.

Essa, E. 2007. *Introduction to early childhood education.* Clifton Park, NY: Delmar Learning.

Fauth, B. 1990. Linking the visual arts with drama, movement, and dance for the young child. In *Moving and learning for the young child* (pp. 159-187), edited by W.J. Stinson. Reston, VA: AAHPERD.

Freedman, D.S., L.K. Khan, W.H. Dietz, S.R. Srinivason, and G.S. Berenson. 2001. Relationship of childhood obesity to coronary heart disease risk factors in adulthood: The Bogalusa heart study. *Pediatrics* 108(3): 712-718.

French, R., L. Silliman, and H. Henderson. 1990. Too much time out. *Strategies* 3: 5-7.

Gallahue, D.L. 1993. *Developmental physical education for today's children.* Dubuque, IA: Brown & Benchmark.

Garcia, C. 1994. Gender differences in young children's interactions when learning fundamental motor skills. *Research Quarterly for Exercise and Sports* 65: 213-225.

Gardner, H. 1993. *Frames of mind: The theory of multiple intelligences.* New York: Basic Books.

Graham, G. 2001. *Teaching children physical education* (2nd ed.). Champaign, IL: Human Kinetics.

Graham, G., S. Holt/Hale, and M. Parker. 2003. *Children moving: A reflective approach to teaching physical education.* Columbus, OH: McGraw-Hill.

Habermeyer, S. 1999. *Good music, brighter children.* Roseville, CA: Prima.

Halsey, E., and L. Porter. 1970. Movement exploration. In *Selected readings in movement education* (pp. 71-77), edited by R.T. Sweeney. Reading, MA: Addison-Wesley.

Hammett, C.T. 1992. *Movement activities for early childhood.* Champaign, IL: Human Kinetics.

Hannaford, C. 2005. *Smart moves: Why learning is not all in your head.* Salt Lake City: Great River Books.

Haubenstricker, J.L., and V. Seefeldt. 2002. The concept of readiness applied to the acquisition of motor skills. In *Children and youth in sport: A biopsychosocial perspective* (pp. 61-81), edited by F.L. Smoll and R.E. Smith. Dubuque, IA: Kendall/Hunt.

Hedley, A.A., C.L. Ogden, C.L. Johnson, M.D. Carroll, L.R. Curtin, and K.M. Flegal. 2004. Prevalence of overweight and obesity among U.S. children, adolescents, and adults, 1999-2002. *Journal of the American Medical Association* 291: 2847-2850.

Hinson, C. 1995. *Fitness for children.* Champaign, IL: Human Kinetics.

Institute for Aerobic Research. 1987. *Get fit.* Dallas: Author.

Institute of Medicine. September, 2006. Progress in preventing childhood obesity: How do we measure up? www.iom.edu/Object.File/Master/36/984/11722_report-brief.pdf.

Jensen, E. 2000a. *Brain-based learning: The new science of teaching and training.* San Diego: The Brain Store.

Jensen, E. 2000b. *Learning with the body in mind: The scientific basis for energizers, movement, play, games, and physical education.* San Diego: The Brain Store.

Katzmarzyk, P.T., L. Pérusse, D.C. Rao, and C. Bouchard. 2000. Familial risk ratios for high and low physical fitness levels in the Canadian population. *Medicine & Science in Sports & Exercise* 32(3): 614-619.

Kirchner, G. 2001. *Physical education for elementary school children.* Columbus, OH: McGraw-Hill.

Klein, J. 1990. Young children and learning. In *Moving and learning for the young child* (pp. 23-30), edited by W.J. Stinson. Reston, VA: AAHPERD.

Kristof, N.D. 1998. Correspondence/uncompetitive in Tokyo; in Japan, nice guys (and girls) finish together. *New York Times,* April 12.

Mayesky, M. 2006. *Creative activities for young children.* Clifton Park, NY: Delmar Learning.

Miller, D.F. 2000. *Positive child guidance.* Clifton Park, NY: Delmar Learning.

Minton, S. 2003. Using movement to teach academics: An outline for success. *Journal of Physical Education, Recreation, and Dance* 74(2): 36-40.

Moore, L.L., U.D.T. Nguyen, K.J. Rothman, L.A. Cupples, and R.C. Ellision. 1995. Preschool physical activity level and chance in body fatness in young children. *American Journal of Epidemiology* 142: 982-988.

Mosston, M., and S. Ashworth. 1990. *The spectrum of teaching styles: From command to discovery.* White Plains, NY: Longman.

Murray, R.L. 1975. *Dance in elementary education.* New York: Harper & Row.

National Association for Sport and Physical Education. 2000. *Appropriate practice in movement programs for young children ages 3-5.* Reston, VA: Author.

National Association for Sport and Physical Education. 2002. *Active start: A statement of physical activity guidelines for children birth to 5 years.* Reston, VA: Author.

National Association for Sport and Physical Education. 2004. *Physical activity for children: A statement of guidelines for children ages 5-12.* Reston, VA: Author.

Ogden, C.L., K.M. Flegal, M.D. Carroll, and C.L. Johnson. 2002. Prevalence and trends in overweight among U.S. children and adolescents, 1999-2000. *Journal of the American Medical Association* 288(14): 1728-1732.

Olds, A.R. 1994. From cartwheels to caterpillars: Children's need to move indoors and out. *Early Childhood Exchange* 97: 32-36.

Orlick, T.D., and R. Mosher. 1978. Extrinsic rewards and participant motivation in a sport-related task. *International Journal of Sport Psychology* 9: 27-39.

Pica, R. 2000. *Moving & learning series: Preschoolers & kindergartners.* Clifton Park, NY: Delmar Learning.

Pica, R. 2001. *Wiggle, giggle, & shake: 200 ways to move and learn.* Beltsville, MD: Gryphon House.

Pica, R. 2006. *Great games for young children: Over 100 games to develop self-confidence, problem-solving skills, and cooperation.* Beltsville, MD: Gryphon House.

President's Council on Physical Fitness and Sports. 2000. Fitness fundamentals. www.hoptechno.com/book11.htm.

Rowen, B. 1982. *Learning through movement.* New York: Teachers College.

Sayre, N., and J. Gallagher. 2001. *The young child and the environment.* Boston: Allyn & Bacon.

Sinclair, C.B. 1973. *Movement of the young child: Ages 2 to 6.* Columbus, OH: Merrill.

Skinner, L. 1979. *Motor development in the preschool years.* Springfield, IL: Thomas.

Sullivan, M. 1982. *Feeling strong, feeling free: Movement exploration for young children.* Washington, DC: National Association for the Education of Young Children.

Thompson, C.E., and L.M. Wankel. 1980. The effects of perceived activity choice upon frequency of exercise behavior. *Journal of Applied Social Psychology* 10: 436-443.

Index

Note: The italicized *f* and *t* following page numbers refer to figures and tables, respectively.

About the Author

Rae Pica, BS, has been a children's physical activity specialist since 1980. A former adjunct instructor with the University of New Hampshire, she is the author of 17 books, including *Experiences in Movement,* the award-winning *Great Games for Young Children,* and *A Running Start: How Play, Physical Activity, and Free Time Create a Successful Child,* written for the parents of children ages birth to 8.

Rae is known for her lively and informative workshop and keynote presentations and has shared her expertise with such groups as the *Sesame Street* research department, the Head Start Bureau, Centers for Disease Control and Prevention, the President's Council on Physical Fitness and Sports, Nickelodeon's *Blue's Clues,* Gymboree, and state health departments throughout the country. She is author of the blog The Pica Perspective, in which she shares her thoughts on matters related to children and physical activity, and is the host and cocreator of Body, Mind and Child, a series of podcasts that help parents prepare their children's minds and bodies for life. In her spare time, she enjoys reading, crocheting, and cheering on the New England Patriots.

*You'll find
other outstanding
physical education resources at*

www.HumanKinetics.com

In the U.S. call

1-800-747-4457

Australia............................. 08 8372 0999
Canada 1-800-465-7301
Europe...................... +44 (0) 113 255 5665
New Zealand........................ 0800 222 062

HUMAN KINETICS
The Information Leader in Physical Activity & Health
P.O. Box 5076 • Champaign, IL 61825-5076 USA